D1546813

How Much Are These Free Books?

True Tales from the Book Nook

Judy S. Hoff

Print book ISBN: 9798988367802
Ebook ISBN: 9798988367819

LCCN: 2023910395

SCHELLINGER ❧ PRESS
Niskayuna, NY

To Larry

CONTENTS

Contents

PREFACE

MOST book-lovers dream of owning their own bookstores. I know this because practically every customer who entered the Book Nook would, sooner or later, pause in their perusal of books, look longingly around, sigh, and say, "I've always dreamed of owning a bookstore."

I owned the Book Nook, a small, independent bookstore for nineteen years, and I loved every minute of it. Well, almost every minute. The job of remaining competitive became difficult. Mail order companies; chain stores; and big box stores—Walmart, Target, and B.J.'S—even grocery stores and drugstores; and especially, the mega bookstores—Borders and Barnes and Noble—and the on-line giant Amazon, often sold books at less than their marked cover price. The cruelest blow came in 1992 when an independent children's bookstore opened just three short blocks away. Children's books were a specialty of mine, dear to my heart, and the new competition threatened to deal the Book Nook a financial death blow.

Yet, the majority of the time, I dashed down to the store each morning, eager to discuss and sell books to my customers. As you flip through these pages — or swipe your devices — I hope you can step back into the days of the Book Nook in Schenectady, New York (1983-2002) and share the joy of bookselling.

"Did you just want to poke around today, or may I help you find something?"

1. Free Books on Fridays

"What is Jane Austen doing in the Free Box?" A customer demanded in horror.

"Well, the book has been highlighted throughout, plus there are a couple of ripped pages. I really didn't feel right sell —"

"Jane Austen should NEVER be in the Free Box!"

"FREE" is a magical word in retailing. When people first saw the new sign, they had difficulty accepting it at face value. They'd march into my tiny used bookstore and ask incredulously, "Those books in that box out there, are they really free?"

"Yes. Help yourself."

"*All* the books in that carton are free?"

"Yes."

They'd mull that over; then blurt out, "Why?"

"Because this is a wonderful store."

The truth was that I was floundering in my first year in business, trying to find a way to boost revenue. Most of the paperbacks looked almost new, but there were some rejects—not in good enough condition to put out on the shelves, yet not musty or tattered enough to throw out. I thought book-lovers might still appreciate these if they were priced low enough. However, I hadn't found takers for them at any price—even for as low as a nickel apiece. About to mark them down to a penny each, it occurred to me that since I was virtually giving them away, why not do the job properly. I lugged a carton of these books outside, dropped it on a folding chair, and stuck a sign on it, announcing:

BOOKS IN THIS BOX ARE FREE ON FRIDAYS

Passers-by were so excited about the free books you'd think I was giving away bars of gold. They'd come inside the store clutching a treasure they'd found in the box and begin a routine worthy of Abbott and Costello's *Who's On First.*

"How much do I owe you for this free book?"

"Nothing, it's free."

"But how much?"

Drawn by the Free Book Box on Fridays, several people also came into the store and browsed, seldom leaving empty-handed. Very few took a free book without at least ducking their heads in the store and thanking me.

Some customers just could not bring themselves to accept something for nothing.

"I've taken this wonderful dictionary from your free box. Can it really be completely free?" The fact that it was missing pages q through z didn't seem to detract from its value in the beholder's eyes.

"Yes, it is."

"Well, then, let me look around here, and I'll find a little something else to buy."

"That's not necessary." Nice, of course, but not necessary.

"I insist."

Sometimes, we'd engage in a bizarre form of dickering.

"Here's fifty cents for this book, *How to Cure Corns,* that I picked up out of that Friday box outside."

"No, no. It's free."

"Seventy-five cents then."

"It's really free."

"Please, I'm going to pay you a buck for it, and that's that. Remember, 'The customer is always right'."

How could I argue with that?

Youngsters walking home from the Howe Elementary School just a block away were the only ones who immediately accepted the word "free." Even though there usually weren't any children's books in the box, they still sounded as excited as if their principal had declared a Snow Day. "Hey, these books are free. *All right!*"

They'd agonize over which book their parent might like, sometimes checking with me for an opinion. "Do you think my mother would rather have *How to Clean Closets More Efficiently* or *Sex God of the Nile?*"

More than one person told me that they were visiting the store because their nine-year-old wouldn't stop nagging them until they had checked out "that really great store that gives away free books."

Initially, I had thought some greedy soul would empty out the box early in the day, and that I would have to put a sign up limiting one book per customer. Instead, just the opposite happened.

"Do you mind if I take two free books this week?"

"Take all you want. Take some more."

"No, I feel guilty taking more than one, as it is. Must leave some for others, you know."

We seldom had a problem finding books for the free box. On the contrary, instead of weeding out defective ones through giving them away, because of well-meaning customers, it became a huge struggle to keep them from multiplying. Practically everybody assured me they'd bring back the free books after they'd read them, or they'd proudly announce they had plenty of books at home, designated for "your free box." I had to plead with customers not to give us any more damaged books since we were running out of space.

We kept the popular Friday carton for a few years. As the inventory of new books increased, however, we had to abandon our free books.

I wasn't sorry to stop selling used books and concentrate instead solely on new ones; but I did miss the Free Book Box and hearing the inevitable question at least once every Friday:

"How much are these free books?"

2. From Typist to Bookstore Owner in Two Months, Part I

(Telephone call from my mother in mid-September 1983)

"Your father and I have talked it over. If this is what you really want, we'll lend you $4000. You do know, though, that in the bookstore business you will not make much money?"

IN the summer of 1983, the thought of opening a bookstore never crossed my mind. I just wanted a different job than the boring clerk-typist one that I held with the New York State Department of Social Services in Albany. When I had first started in the position, I had intended for it to be a temporary one—two months at the most—until another job opened up with the State more in line with my college education. I was hoping for a position such as the one I had when working in New York City for the State as an interviewer and then as a supervisor, from 1965 until 1970, when I left to have our first child.

Shortly after I became a clerk-typist in the early 1980s, a hiring freeze crushed my plans for a more professional State job. Because I dreaded facing job interviews and liked the people with whom I worked, after more than two years as a clerk typist, I was still just drifting along that summer of 1983.

The morning after Labor Day, however, I was reassigned out of the small prime unit into a unit of eight people, each of whom thought his or her forms and memos should be completed, not in the order in which they were placed in my in-basket, but before everybody else's. It was type, type, type practically the same words over and over all day long. Yes, it was what I was paid to do, but within a week, I knew I wouldn't keep my sanity if I stayed.

My husband and I talked over what I could do instead. We scoured want ads, but nothing looked promising. Larry kept asking me, "What do you really want to do?"

I finally said, "Of course, my dream job would be owning a bookstore, but that's an impractical fantasy, not really feasible."

We had both often said Upper Union Street in Schenectady needed a bookstore, but both of us meant it would be an ideal place for someone else to open a bookstore, someone who had experience selling books.

Neither one of us had envisioned me as being the one to do it.

Yet the seed was suddenly planted.

Larry said it wouldn't hurt to investigate. Was there even a place to rent at a reasonable price?

We found there was a small store at a modest rent in the middle of a short block at 1606 Union Street. It was also just a ten-minute walk from our home, which meant that our two daughters, then in fourth and eighth grade, could easily come visit me at the store.

But what about inventory? I spent a weekend exploring yard sales and found that there were plenty of used books available at bargain prices.

The idea of opening up a used bookstore had taken root in our minds. But weren't there many complicated government hoops to go through first? I consulted a lawyer and found out there were only two simple requirements to open a bookstore:

1. Obtain a $25 DBA (doing business as) certificate from Schenectady County.
2. Acquire an employer number from the Internal Revenue Service.

So far, aside from the lawyer's fee, we hadn't spent any money in our explorations, but if I were to go forward, it was crunch time. We had no extra cash, however, to open a business. Zero. Zip. Zilch.

I called my parents and explained about our investigations into the possibility of opening a used bookstore in Schenectady, that everything seemed aligned for me to open a store, except for this one little problem . . .

After considering it overnight, my mother called me back the next day and said they would lend me the money.

Suddenly, I had the cash to proceed. Knowing nothing about running a bookstore and having no retailing experience, I plunged blindly ahead.

3. From Typist to Bookstore Owner in Two Months, Part II

Overheard at my job with the State: "Why is the typist in our unit suddenly smiling all the time?"

IN the last week of September, 1983, I signed a two year lease for the tiny store at 1606 Union Street that I planned to open as a used bookshop. I gleefully turned in my notice at the State. My daughters remember me singing, *"Toot, Toot, Tootsie, Good-bye"* as I served out my remaining time there.

Every weekend that fall, I cruised yard sales, picking out books for inventory. Some homeowners, once they found out I was going to open a bookstore, reduced their prices and a few even went inside their homes and brought out more books for me to inspect. I only picked up used books in mint condition. While paying 25 to 50 cents for other paperbacks, I soon learned that I shouldn't go over a dime apiece for the plentiful Harlequin romances. Science fiction books seemed scarce; mysteries more plentiful.

I visited a used paperback bookstore in Delmar, more than a half hour's drive from Schenectady. Once the owner realized I wasn't planning to open a store across the street from her, she generously gave me invaluable advice. She named the wholesaler she used for her few new books, suggested I sign up with the ABA (American Booksellers Association), and explained her store's used book pricing policy. With ABA membership, I purchased their thick *Bookselling Manual*, which I read cover to cover so many times it became tattered.

I also drove north two and a half hours one day to Lake Placid to meet with the owner of a used bookstore there. She gave me more valuable advice. Her biggest tip was to warn me to save enough to pay the sales tax due every three months. Apparently, that first bill had been an unpleasant surprise for her.

Bookcases were a problem. The professional ones were prohibitively expensive. Luckily, one weekend we visited Larry's family at their home in North Creek, near the popular Gore Mountain Ski Resort. Their neighbor did carpentry and agreed to build our bookcases. Larry had meticulously measured and determined we needed 11 seven-foot-tall bookcases, ranging from thirty inches to forty-eight inches wide.

The carpenter used Adirondack white pine, stained the cases maple, and brought them down in his truck for us — all for $40 a bookcase.

I ordered stationery and an outdoor sign with red lettering and a white background for the store. Because of the store's miniature size, we thought the name "Book Nook" would be appropriate. AT&T gave me a horribly non-memorable telephone number. I protested, and the representative claimed I only had two more tries for a better number. Fortunately, on the next attempt, the number offered was 518-346-0075. Since many in the area already had the 346 exchange, most customers would only have to remember the 0075 part, so I gratefully grabbed that number.

Larry, as a salesman for the Hobart Kitchen Equipment Company, told all his restaurant dealers about my new adventure, and they proved very generous with book donations and supplies. One of his dealers donated a red comfortable chair to go with the rectangular white desk that I had purchased; another dealer gave us a dish cart that worked well as a rolling book cart.

Chuck and Millie Eisenberg, an older couple, both very short in stature with round cherubic faces, owned the variety store on Upper Union Street. They gave me much needed retailing advice. Chuck emphasized that customers only saw the two shelves at eye level, usually nothing above or below. Those two shelves were where

I should place books face out that I wanted customers to notice the most. Millie warned against making displays too meticulous, since customers would be reluctant to disturb them. I reassured her she didn't have to worry about my being too neat. They both emphasized that if a customer actually reached for a book and held it in his or her hands, the chances of a sale increased significantly.

Although not one to flaunt his own strengths, Larry urged me to make the store name and my own name prominent by doing the following:

1. Order business cards with the store address and phone number as well as including my name as "bookseller."
2. Answer the phone with my last name, too, not just my first. *"Book Nook, Judy Hoff speaking."*
3. Promote the store and myself everywhere.

While the first two actions could be implemented immediately, the third kept evolving over several years.

Even though the store's main inventory of used books did not lend itself to a big holiday business in December, I hustled to open the store as soon as possible to take advantage of the season since I had also ordered a small selection of new books. My first display on a bridge table covered by a red cloth contained:

1. The hardcover bestseller, *Poland*, by James Michener.

2. The hardcover bestseller, *Pet Semetary*, by Stephen King.
3. The paperback, *Space*, by James Michener.
4. The newly released non-fiction book, *O Albany*, by William Kennedy, a local author who was becoming well-known nationally.
5. The Albany Trilogy of trade paperback novels: *Ironweed*, *Legs*, and *Billy Phelan's Last Game*, by William Kennedy.
6. A cookbook.
7. A knitting book.

Squeezed in, too, on that table was the classic novel, *1984*, by George Orwell, first published forty years before. Since January of 1984 was fast approaching, everyone wanted to read the book again to see how close to reality the predictions were. It bore some resemblance to totalitarian countries, but it still seemed too weird to apply to a democracy like the United States even forty years after it was written. Of course, from the point of view of the second decade of the twenty-first century, it now seems more ominous.

At Larry's suggestion, I had written to Isaac Nichols, an artist we had met at a New England craft fair. He sent me eleven framed wooden numbered prints of his small pen and ink drawings of Vermont scenes. I took them on consignment, and we hung them about the store.

We planned a well-advertised grand opening for December 3, 1983, complete with a wine and cheese party, but I quietly opened my doors on November 19th, so I could slowly get used to taking care of customers. This head start was crucial since there was so much I didn't know about bookselling.

4. BECOMING A REAL BOOKSTORE

Several people used the Book Nook as their midpoint reward for exercise – either walking or biking – telling me firmly when they entered that they had purposely left their wallet at home so they wouldn't be tempted to buy anything. "I'm just looking today if that's okay?" "Of course," I responded, "browsing is good." It was easy to be gracious because I knew it would be only a matter of minutes before the "just looking" person would sheepishly approach my desk with a pile of books. "Do you mind putting these aside for me, while I go home for my money?"

WHEN the Book Nook opened on November 19, 1983, not many gave the store much chance of success. Looking around at the eleven bookcases containing used paperbacks and hardcovers acquired through yard sales and donations, and the one bridge table with a few new bestsellers perched on top, I really couldn't blame them. If customers wanted to browse, they kept looking uneasily at me as I sat at my desk in the middle of the store. The desk served as the sales counter. I tried to make them feel less under surveillance by studying a book catalog, but in just 200 square feet, it was tricky to become invisible.

Many people, men especially, would step up the two stairs into the store, look around, and comment, "I bet we have more books in our living room than you do in your whole store. Ha. Ha." I smiled at them as if they were as witty as Johnny Carson, but I ranted at home. "I swear if just *one* more person says that to me, I am going to grab Michener's hardcover, *Poland,* and beat him over the head with it!"

Even though we were primarily a used bookstore, and used bookstores usually do not do well during the December holiday time, so many people came in looking for new books as gifts that I kept re-ordering more books from our wholesaler.

Occasionally, someone would come in, glance around disdainfully, and ask, "Ma'am, could you direct me to a *real* bookstore?"

That hurt.

Yet, it was also amazing how supportive the majority of people who stopped in were. They made positive comments such as:

"The store is just charming."

"For such a tiny store, you have the most wonderful selection."

"I appreciate your taking the trouble to order just a paperback and get it so quickly."

I wish I could report that it came naturally to go above and beyond in terms of service, but it took a customer, who overheard me dismissing someone on the phone, to guide me toward the right path.

"Judy, what did you just do?"

"Told a customer we didn't have a book."

"And?"

"I offered to order it for him," I said self-righteously, "but he didn't want to wait for it."

"And what did he ask that you said you didn't know?"

"He asked if I knew where he could get it?"

"Yes. He particularly came to you first. You should have told him you'd find out for him and call around other bookstores until you found a copy or were sure there were none in the area and call him back to report to him either way. Do you think maybe next time he wanted a book, he'd try you first again?"

As much as it pained me to admit it, he was right.

Just three weeks after we opened and a few months before he won the Pulitzer Prize for *Ironweed*, I had written to area author, William Kennedy. I mentioned that his newly released *O Albany*, a non-fiction book with the descriptive subtitle: *Improbable City of Political Wizards, Fearless Ethnics, Spectacular Aristocrats, Splendid Nobodies, and Underrated Scoundrels*, was the first new book I had ordered for the store. I asked him if he could come sign copies. In January I heard back from him. He couldn't do an autograph session, but he would be glad to sign copies of his books if I brought them to his house.

Of course!

I swallowed hard and ordered twenty copies each of the trade paperback trilogy novels, *Ironweed*, *Legs,* and *Billy Phelan's Greatest Game,* plus thirty hardcover copies of *O Albany.* I longed to order many more, but didn't dare get in over my head with excessive inventory costs.

My husband and I carted the books early one January Monday morning out to the Kennedys' home. Since I had to return to open the store, we had a very enjoyable, but necessarily short visit with the author and his gracious wife, Dana. After inquiring about a couple of Albany's colorful political figures and listening to delightful anecdotes relating to them, I watched the author sign one after another of his books. The chore looked tedious, and I asked if he were tired of signing books yet.

"Are you kidding!" he answered with a big grin.

When I returned to the store, I found multiple answering machine messages asking if any William Kennedy books were available. The day before, the Sunday *New York Times* had featured a very favorable review about his latest book, *O Albany,* and praised his novels.

This was actually the *one* time in all my years of bookselling where I had on hand an unexpected demand book. Not only did I have it on hand, but I had multiple signed copies, when all the other booksellers in the area were out of stock. It was a prime example of beginner's luck.

Those thirty *O Albany* copies and twenty each of the *Ironweed Trilogy* did not last long.

Customers began returning to browse and to buy on a regular basis. The telephone rang with requests for orders. I couldn't believe how loyal some customers became. They easily could have picked up a bestseller at the supermarket or picked up a mystery when they were browsing in another bookstore, but they conscientiously copied down titles and called me up to order them. Or, instead of mail ordering an art book from a museum catalog, they would give the Book Nook a call.

Several bought our gift certificates. "It'll be a good way to introduce my neighbor to your store. She loves to read and might become a good customer for you."

After the first three months in business, my husband drew up floor plans to enlarge the Book Nook. We purchased eight more bookcases for the used books again from the carpenter in North Creek. Soon after, we splurged and bought two more professional bookcases from a furniture supplier, placing them length-wise in the center of the store to hold new books. These were shorter than our original ones and had slanted shelves so some titles could easily be placed face out. We also moved my desk toward the back. Anyone with a question or anyone who was ready to pay would have to go by a tantalizing display of books to get to me. As I had hoped, titles seemed to scream out as customers passed: *Pick me up; you're going to love me!*

Even doubling its space to 400 square feet, however, the size of the store could still only be described as very small.

One day when a harried-looking man learned we were out of the very popular business book by Peters and Waterman, *In Search of Excellence*, he asked, "Are there any other bookstores nearby?"

As I named the closest bookstores and also asked if he'd like me to call them for him, and mentioned my replacement order of the book was due in the very next day, I realized that no one had asked for a "real bookstore" in months.

In the public's view, the Book Nook had become a legitimate bookshop.

5. BOOKLOVERS' HEAVEN: MY FIRST AMERICAN BOOKSELLERS' CONVENTION

(Telephone call to my parents after my ABA visit, Spring 1984)

My father: Hi, Jude. How's it going? Did you do anything over the weekend?

Me, trying to be very nonchalant: I did actually. I had breakfast Sunday with Lee Iacocca and Rosalyn Carter.

A TTENDING my first American Booksellers Association (ABA) Convention in Washington, D. C. in the spring of 1984, I felt a little like Orphan Annie when she first entered Daddy Warbucks's mansion. Only the knowledge that I couldn't carry a tune kept me from bursting into song *(I think I'm going to like it here.)*. The glitz, the glamor, and the circus atmosphere reminded me of that scene in the play, too. And there were all those wonderful people in the book business gathered there from all around the world.

Since it was a last-minute decision to attend, I didn't realize there was a seminar to orient first timers. I scurried around looking at books and trying to find the autograph sessions of famous authors, such as Gloria Stenem, Belva Plain, and Helen Hayes. These celebrities were gracious as I gushed about how thrilling it was to obtain autographed copies of their books and would they just sign it please in place of putting in my name.

Instead of treasuring these stars' books, I planned to sell them in my bookstore in order to make some money to justify the expense of the trip to Washington D.C. I hadn't intended going to the convention until two days before when my husband learned of it and argued—correctly as it turned out—that attendance was a professional necessity.

Workshops were very informative, as was talking to more experienced booksellers. One lecturer particularly drove home the importance of controlling inventory costs. Right then, I resolved to set a limit for monthly buying and to stick rigidly to it. No exceptions.

Ha! In almost nineteen years in business I struggled the entire time to refrain from ordering too many books, but it was like putting an alcoholic in a liquor store. Title after title called to me. The problem, of course, was whether it was a good bookselling month or a slow one, wholesalers and publishers still expected to be paid.

As I traveled up and down the aisles, gathering catalogs and free books along the way, my sore arms and aching feet were the only reminders that my body was still on this earth and that I hadn't been transported to booksellers' heaven.

It was a bit intimidating to wander about and overhear an occasional buyer from one of the chains say to a salesman, "I'll take 50 copies of those, 200 of those . . . " In contrast, my first question of every sales rep at each booth where I was tempted to buy was, "What's your minimum order?"

Nonetheless, many salespeople, spotting my blue badge denoting a bookseller, treated me with the eagerness of a New Hampshire primary politician discovering a real voter among the media masses.

Reps asks where Schenectady was located, and when they learned it was near Albany, New York, most immediately identified it as "William Kennedy Territory." He had just won the Pulitzer prize for *Ironweed* earlier that spring, and was one of the reasons the Book Nook survived its first year in business. The enormous local and national publicity about him helped sell his books for us.

The aisles at the ABA, featuring large publishers, such as Random House and St. Martin's, were so crowded I didn't even attempt to go down them. I moseyed around Ingram's booths, our sole wholesaler at the time, since I had such warm feelings toward them.

At least two or three times a week, I talked to their friendly Tennessee order-takers. ("*The Book Nook from Schenectady? How much snow do you all have on the ground?*") I also discovered several small presses with interesting titles.

Assuming it would be awkward to go alone, I hadn't intended to go to the author breakfasts. A bookselling couple from Arizona, however, who joined me at the crowded cafeteria for lunch on the first day, urged me to go to every author event possible. "The best part is talking to other booksellers."

They were right. Not only booksellers, but publishers, wholesalers, agents, librarians, and book club people attended the breakfasts. These events provided insights into the publishing and bookselling business.

Rosalyn Carter and Lee Iacocca, both authors of forthcoming autobiographies were the feature speakers at my first ABA breakfast. Studs Terkel, the announcer, mentioned in his introduction what an ordeal public speaking used to be for Rosalyn Carter and even then, after four years as First Lady, she still visibly trembled before she began speaking. As she began talking, however, she relaxed and gave an entertaining speech about the difficulties of transition from First Lady to ordinary citizen. She referred to the discipline needed to write, to actually sit down each day and put words on paper.

Rosalyn Carter received a standing ovation before she spoke, Lee Iacocca received one after he spoke, which was not surprising, considering the line with which the ultimate salesman finished as he asked for the order. "You stock my book when it comes out next fall, and I guarantee you I will sell it for you."

It was a memorable breakfast, one with which I could share with my customers. Even after I explained there were several hundred other people present as well, they still seem intrigued.

When I had these celebrities' books in the store — unsigned since the autographed ones sold immediately — if someone so much as glanced in their direction, I seized the opportunity to mention. "Yes, Rosalyn Carter — Gloria Steinem, Helen Hayes or Belva Plain -- is a lovely person. When I saw her last May at the American Bookseller's Convention . . . "

Or, "Lee Iacocca is such a stimulating speaker. No wonder he sells so many cars."

Such shameless name-dropping did get customers' attention and even sold books.

And from then on my husband shared in the fun, accompanying me to the ABA Conventions. After each convention, I suspected that during his business calls he did a little name-dropping of his own.

6. Learning, or Why a Waldenbooks' Employee Sent Customers to the Book Nook

A well-dressed woman came into the store, announcing she had a $20 gift certificate.

"That's always fun" I said, but it didn't turn out to be fun for me – until the end.

She was on a mission to spend $20. Not a penny more. Not a penny less. No matter how long it took. What's more she involved me in her mission. "How much would these be?" she asked, plunking down a few books on my desk, "Put in the sales tax, too." $10 and change. She brought more books over, having me add them in, one at a time, refiguring the tax each time – with a calculator because I didn't have a cash register yet.

Then, she saw the special sale of used romance paperbacks that were 80% off the cover price instead of 50% off as the others were, so she had me subtract out five books and add back in romances, one at a time. Finally, she reached $20. Except it was over at $21.50. She took a book out and replaced it with a cheaper one. We were still over $20 again, this time *at $20.56. I caved and said, "Let's call it an even $20."She liked that and handed me the gift certificate.*

I glanced at it and did a double take. "I'm sorry. This is not the Book Nook's gift certificate. This is for the bookstore downtown, The Open Door."

MOST people enter a used bookstore with the expectation of saving money. That's understandable. What aggravated me, however, was the small minority of customers (perhaps ten percent), who came in determined not only to find bargains, but to chisel me down to the last available penny.

They argued about everything.

1. Why wasn't I giving them money for their family Bible? It was probably worth a fortune. They ignored my comment that most people carefully preserved their family Bibles, so unless it was the Gutenberg, it was probably too common to be worth anything. Besides, I didn't give money, I only gave credit to buy used books.

2. Why was I giving them only 20% exchange credit for paperbacks? They acted as if I were gouging them. Despite the signs showing the sale price of 50% or less off the cover price of used paperbacks, they somehow retained in

their minds the full original cover price as my selling price.

3. Why was I rejecting so many of their paperbacks for credit? I was much too particular.

- Too musty? Clean them.
- Ripped pages? Scotch tape them.
- Already have too many of their titles? Get inventive.

These few contentious traders did not contribute to the calm atmosphere I wanted to create in the Book Nook, and out of desperation, I established a new procedure that the store would accept no more than twenty books at a time for credit. This made negotiations remarkably better. These customers may not have been less quarrelsome, but at least we conducted these fierce debates over a much shorter time period.

For the majority of customers who brought in paperbacks in popular categories in near mint condition, I made "an exception" and repealed the twenty book rule. The more books they brought in, the better.

To my surprise, it turned out to be harder to sell used hardcovers than paperbacks, no matter how low the selling price. Therefore, I stopped accepting hardcovers.

I began to know my customers. One voracious reader, D.C., came in about every third day with a bunch of paperbacks in mint condition to exchange. He read every genre except romance — and would even read those titles if they were the only available reading material. He was a particular fan of Elmore Leonard, and to my customer's delight the author had suddenly gained major acclaim. Leonard's books moved from the narrower westerns and the suspense genres into popular mainstream fiction. Mr. L., another customer — a white-haired, very courtly gentleman with whom, unlike most of my customers, I never became on a first name basis — placed frequent orders with me, but insisted he did not want to be called when his book came; he'd just stop in when it was due to arrive. Eventually, he confessed his wife disapproved of his book buying habit.

As my business grew, I started ordering books for the store with specific customers in mind and also began to trust my own tastes. If I thought a coffee table book looked appealing, chances were so would my customers, or if I particularly enjoyed a novel, many of my customers would too.

From the first month of business, if we didn't have a requested book on hand, I encouraged customers to order books, no matter whether it was an expensive art book or an inexpensive paperback.

A Waldenbooks' employee, who lived near the Book Nook, stopped in one day to check the store out. We began talking, and she gave me the titles of books about the British Royal family that were only available directly from publishers. Ordering from a publisher was a slower and more labor intensive process than the normal ordering process from a wholesaler. Could I get these books for her? Apparently, Walden's individual stores sent all orders to their headquarters first, adding an extra step to the process. The chances of an individual order that was not immediately available from Walden's major wholesaler actually arriving were less than if the order were placed in Tibet. Incidentally, practically all bookstores, including very small stores such as mine, used the same major wholesaler, Ingram. The big difference was that when customers ordered from the Book Nook, instead of a larger store, they placed the order with me, the person who would also order their books directly from Ingram and who would also be aware of when the order would actually arrive — at that time about two days. It was the same process with orders from publishers, but, unlike Walden employees who had no clue about the ordering process, I warned customers it would take two weeks, maybe much longer.

Soon, to my surprise, disgruntled Waldenbooks' customers began showing up at the Book Nook, saying skeptically they were referred by an employee there who said I was an expert at obtaining special orders.

It was a pleasure to prove her right.

Unfortunately, not all Walden's customers became fans of the Book Nook. One woman started out very negatively, not liking the one new dictionary I had on hand, *The Lincoln's Writer's Dictionary*, but she agreed to order a Webster's children's paperback. She, like most parents, ignored my opinion that, at least by fifth grade, children should have regular dictionaries because there is nothing more discouraging to a child, I would imagine, than to look up a word and not find it in a limited children's dictionary. She did take another look at the *Lincoln* dictionary and conceded "This one is not bad actually, but he needs one to carry back and forth to school." I said, "Just a thought, but if you got both, you could keep one at home, and order the paperback for his backpack."

She surprised me by saying, "That's what I'll do. I've got three kids who can use this one at home." So she bought the $17.95 dictionary and ordered the $4.95 one. I told myself that's the result when I "ask for the order."

A couple of days later, she came back. She wanted to return *The Lincoln Writing Dictionary* and said she didn't want the paperback dictionary that I had ordered for her either. She had purchased a dictionary at Walden's she liked better than either of my recommendations. So much for my great salesmanship. What's more, she left before I remembered to ask for the title of the dictionary she did buy from Walden's.

7. Experimenting

One afternoon during a quiet spell in the Book Nook, I decided to duck out and pick up soup for my lunch from Gershon's Deli, three doors away. As I was locking my front door, something made me glance back through the display window; and to my shocked disbelief there was one of my most frequent customers, D.C., checking out the used paperback mysteries. Of course, I immediately re-opened the door with profuse apologies.

"No, problem," he said with a laugh. "That's always been one of my dreams to be locked inside of a bookstore."

He volunteered to watch the store while I went out to pick up my soup and claimed I had returned much too quickly.

IN the spring during the Book Nook's first year, I experimented with staying open late Friday nights, thinking people might want to pick up reading material after work for the weekend, but there were few customers. Larry and the girls often brought pizza in on these Fridays so we could all have supper together. One lonely Friday evening, however, when my family had stayed home, I peeked into a customer's book that had come in that afternoon. I had called the customer, mentioning that the store was open late that night, but he said he'd pick it up first thing Saturday morning. I don't recall the title, but it was a marketing book, not nearly as meaty as *Guerrilla Marketing* by Jay Levinson, but it did contain a few interesting tips. I reached for a pen and paper to take notes, being careful to hold the pages at an angle so they wouldn't get pressed down.

A little while later—this was before my husband attached a row of bells on the front door that jingled when someone entered—I looked up to see a man looming over my desk. He was glaring at his open book and my notetaking in full disapproval mode. I jumped about a foot, turned red, smiled weakly and said, "Er-uhm-ah-so sorry. You caught me." Lips tightly sealed, he paid and stomped out.

In contrast, many customers were surprisingly generous about sharing their ordered books with me, urging "Take a look at my novel when it comes in, I think you'll like it." A few even went as far as to suggest I take their book home and read it first. I never took them up on their generous offer, since my priority was to get books moving out of the store and cash in the till as quickly as possible.

After a few months I abandoned the late night hours except for the December holiday season. It did show me, however, that customers liked to stop in on their way home from work, and I extended my closing time from five-thirty to six.

Customers became increasingly protective of the Book Nook. For instance, when a woman barged past another customer to pick up her order, I was about to say, "I am sorry but this person was here first." The customer, however, gave me a definite shake of her head, indicating that she preferred to wait, rather than create a disturbance. Oblivious to this by-play, The *Trouble-Maker* said loudly to me, "How is your store doing? When you first opened I gave you two months, but you've lasted three years. I don't understand it because Schenectady is a complete cultural wasteland. It isn't as if it's a college town."

"Come on," I said. "There's Union College that was chartered as the first non-denominational institution in the United States and Schenectady Com—"

"That doesn't count. Union's a bunch of engineers who never read, and the professors are the worst as far as reading goes." Having insulted S. W., the college professor behind her, who was so patiently waiting to buy three novels, she went on to insult even more customers. "Of course there's GE which is the only thing in this town, and you *know* they never read."

"I have a lot of GE customers who read," I contradicted her. Two of them I cringed to see were in the store listening to our conversation.

"No," she insisted, "it's an intellectual wasteland in Schenectady."

"I object to that statement," a gray-haired woman spoke up. She belonged to a book group that wanted to read the *Odyssey*, but they were waiting for the Lattimore translation. No other translation would do, and half of the members would have preferred to read it in the original Greek.

Thankfully, *The Trouble-Maker* didn't continue making provocative statements. She paid for her book, *The Last Word of the Gentle Art of Verbal Self-Defense,* and left.

What amused me the most about the ensuing dissection of *The Trouble-Maker* was that the participants weren't antagonized by her disparaging their own professions, but angry on behalf of the Book Nook. I may have missed something, but I didn't think she was denigrating the Book Nook, other than surprised we were still open in such a supposedly intellectual wasteland.

Trying to insert an element of fun for customers, I often gave discounts on Valentine's Day for any books with red on the cover or on St. Patrick's day for any books with green on the cover. During one of the store's earliest years, I posted a sign in the front window quoting a different opening line of a classic each Friday. (*It was the best of times, it was the worst of times.*) Those who recognized the book title received a discount off their purchases that day. Of course, in later years when cell phones became more prevalent, that quiz wouldn't have worked since anyone would be able to pull up the answer by the time they walked in the front door.

Publishers, especially children's publishers, sent booksellers promotional items, such as bookmarks, bookplates, and lovely illustrated posters, and I passed these items on to teachers and librarians.

And then, there were the silly things I shared with some customers such as the dedication in a used hardcover book. The only thing I recall about the contents of the book was that its main focus was animals and it was dedicated to the author's husband and her dogs. I have long since forgotten the title and the name of the husband and the dogs, so I invented the names in the following dedication. I haven't forgotten their order, however, which resulted in many pithy comments from my customers about the husband's importance — or lack of it — in that household.

To Rufus and Spot

and

to my husband, John

8. WILL THE REAL MIA FARROW PLEASE STAND UP

Sometime during the court trial when Mia Farrow was trying to keep her youngest child from being alone with Woody Allen, her mother, Maureen O'Sullivan Cushing — most famous for her role as Jane to Johnny Weissmuller's Tarzan — called the store.

"This is Maureen Cushing, I'd like the Woody Allen book. I don't suppose you have it in?

"No, I'm sorry, Mrs. Cushing."

"Good. That's good, but please order it for me."

"Certainly. Would you like the hardcover or the paperback edition?"

"Oh, paperback definitely." She paused. "It should be toilet paper actually." She giggled, adding, "I suppose I shouldn't have said that."

"I can see where you might feel that way, Mrs. Cushing."

I N Amagansett, which was part of the town of East Hampton, New York, where I grew up during the nineteen forties and fifties, practically every other person we bumped into, especially in the summer season, was a celebrity. And this was before the Hamptons became ultra popular and glitzy.

My father drilled water wells for Dick Cabot, Roger Caras, and Robert De Niro among others; he also did plumbing work for Jackson Pollack. My mother typed the manuscript of *Letting Go* for Philip Roth. I babysat for the daughters of the television writer, David Shaw; and for the son of the artists, Miriam Schapiro and Paul Brach.

Like most locals, we took these celebrities for granted. My grandfather took this nonchalance to extremes, however, when he met the one person every other man in town longed to meet.

When Gramp returned to the plumbing shop in Amagansett one morning, my father asked him, "Where've you been, Pop?"

"Fixing a faucet at one of the cottages at Stony Hill Farm."

Dad became alert at the mention of Stony Hill Farm. After all, everybody had been talking about one of its famous inhabitants for weeks. "Whose faucet?"

"A Mrs. Miller."

Now the town is populated with Millers, but there was only one Miller that mattered at the moment to my father, and she and Arthur Miller were renting one of the cottages at Stony Hill.

"Do you mean *Marilyn Monroe* Miller?"

"Who?"

"Marilyn Monroe. You know, Marilyn Mon-*roe!*"

Grandpa rubbed his chin thoughtfully and eventually nodded. "Must have been."

"How'd she look? Was she pretty? Glamorous? Sexy?"

"Couldn't tell. Had a lot of grease on her face, and her hair was in curlers."

And that was the most detailed description anyone in our family was ever able to drag out of my grandfather about his meeting with one of the most famous and glamorous women in our time.

In contrast, although Schenectady had plenty of visiting celebrities in its heyday, not too many made it into the city in the 1980s.

Mia Farrow did enter the Book Nook once, although I'm sorry to say, I didn't recognize her even when she handed me a credit card with the name "Mia Farrow" on it. At the time the only movie I'd seen in years was "The Black Stallion," which I really enjoyed — much to the disgust of my daughters who were on a campaign to get me to see more sophisticated movies.

Mia, accompanied by her children as well as a woman friend with a toddler, browsed happily in my store for quite a while and collected a big pile of books. When she handed me her charge card, I did recognize the name. But I remembered a skinny, waif-like kid when she had been married to Frank Sinatra more than twenty years earlier. I took one look at this attractive, suburban matron with a full figure and three children in tow, and told myself, "Nah, it has to be another Mia Farrow." As usual, pre-occupied with the books being purchased, I blithely chatted on about one of the paperbacks she was getting about Frank Sinatra and how the paperback was so much less expensive than the hardcover which I didn't have on hand. She looked startled, but I kept rambling on and on. Yes, I know it wasn't as if her card said "Jane Smith" and, yes, the Frank Sinatra book should have clued me in.

Since she and her friend seemed in a shopping and spending mode, I mentioned that there was a gift shop next door, carrying lovely handcrafted items that they might want to check out.

The minute they had closed my front door, and I saw that they were headed for Creations, I called the owner, to warn her not to get too uptight if the friend's child was still eating Rice Krispies and leaving a trail behind him since their purchases might well compensate for the nuisance of clean-up.

Phyllis had immediately sized up the situation. "Can't talk now, Judy." Her store shared the same main entrance as a beauty parlor, and, someone in there spotted Mia as she was leaving Creations, and everyone in the whole shop, ignoring dripping wet hair, drooping curlers, and permanent lotion only half applied, raced to gape as Mia left the building, burdened down with purchases.

I did learn later that her mother, Maureen O'Sullivan, lived in the adjacent town, Niskayuna, and shopped fairly regularly on Upper Union Street. She had in fact, occasionally shopped in my store. When told her married name was Cushing, I was able to place her as that pleasant lady who always asked how the shop was doing and wished me success each time she came in.

During the Mia Farrow – Woody Allen battle a few years later, I became indignant on Mia's behalf when some of the scandal sheets implied that her devoted mother image might be a sham. During just those few minutes that she was in my store, I had observed that she knew her children's literature, since with an unerring eye she had selected the best of my children's books. She obviously read to her children a lot, certainly an important sign of a conscientious mother. Also, one of her children, a handsome boy perhaps in his early teens, brought over a hardcover book and asked her, "Is this too expensive?"

"No," she replied. "I may not buy you other things, but books are something that I will always buy for you."

The woman's love life may have been less than ideal from time to time, but obviously she had her priorities straight when it came to her children.

9. 1987: A Memorable Year

A man came in from a book club that had several other members who frequented my store. It was his first time. "Are you, Maggie?"

"No, I'm Judy Hoff."

"Good," he said. "I thought it was something like that. They told me to ask you to pick out a book for our club. Here's the list they've already chosen. I want a novel." He kept trying to smooth down his gray hair which looked as if he'd forgotten to comb it.

I showed him Updike's RABBIT REDUX and a couple of other books, but strongly suggested Dick Francis' LONGSHOT. "You're safe on this one. The author's very popular, and I know L.W. [One of the fussiest of his book club members] also likes it." I had a particular fondness for the author's English horse racing mysteries myself, especially since my father liked his books, too.

When L.W. came in a few days later, I mentioned to her how the club member had struggled over his decision. Relieved, he'd chosen the Dick Francis book, she explained that in the past whenever it was his turn to select a book, he always chose one everyone else had hated. Several members had begged him this time to consult me. "I'll like it at any rate, and the others at the very least will will see it as a vast improvement over his past selections."

D URING 1987, my business life and my personal life collided.

On the business level, the owners of the building that contained the Book Nook were retiring and moving to Florida. My husband and I decided to buy the building, which also included a now empty, larger store next to the Book Nook and a spacious apartment upstairs. We financed the purchase with about five cents down and two mortgages. By necessity, we became reluctant landlords.

The first renters in the apartment upstairs turned out to be the *Tenants From Hell* – and, yes, I had checked references. Their drama involved a jealous second boyfriend, a sledgehammer through the apartment entryway door, the police, and furniture moved outside to the front of the Book Nook, where a screaming match occurred. In comparison, all later apartment dwellers were a huge improvement.

While the *Tenants From Hell* were wreaking havoc, I continued to operate the Book Nook as usual but was also making plans to move into the larger store next to it. Renovations for the new Book Nook store included hiring professionals to tear down a dividing wall and put in carpeting. I set about wallpapering and painting Sundays and at night when the Book Nook was closed. One Sunday morning I was trying to place red and white windowpane wallpaper on the three-foot overhang along the perimeter of the store, but I couldn't get it to stick except to my hands, making one holy mess. I had to call my husband for help, feeling guilty since he had just returned exhausted from a business trip. In his careful, precise manner, he efficiently hung the wallpaper although I don't think he'd ever done wallpapering before.

I managed the painting quite well on my own—at first. Midway back along the west wall of the store, I painted white the four pillars that had formerly formed a dressing room and red the countertop in front of it. It would now be the pay station. The children's section would go next to the pay station, extending across to the opposite wall where I could keep an eagle eye to prevent little hands from smooshing the pages of expensive hardcover picture books. I painted in bright primary colors several open boxes that were built against that east wall, perfect for displaying children's picture books.

One evening while painting a support beam white, the chair I was standing on tipped over. Yes, I should have been on a ladder. I hit the top of the chair with my mid-section and went down. Fortunately, I was able to get up and didn't seem too badly hurt at the time, but the pain in my middle didn't improve. Eventually I went for X-rays, which revealed three broken ribs. When asked if they would heal, the doctor's reply was, "Yes, if you don't paint any more."

A professional painter finished the job. I had decided on white also for the walls although the nineteen original maple-stained bookcases which we transferred from the old store and placed along the walls covered up most of the new paint job. We also moved the two higher quality bookcases to the middle of the store and purchased two more.

We kept only five bookcases of used books against the east wall in the front section, but within a year these, too, were phased out and replaced by new books. That meant no more tension in giving exchange credit. It also meant I had to pay for all our inventory with actual money, instead of acquiring the used portion of it with exchange credit. Although the larger store gained new customers, regrettably some avid readers like D.C. stopped coming in.

We rented the former Book Nook space to Henry's Dry Cleaning, who wanted a pick-up and drop-off place on Upper Union Street. In contrast to the *Tenants From Hell*, Henry's proved to be a *Dream Tenant*; its customers used the parking spaces in front of the building for only a few minutes — unless they decided to browse in the Book Nook.

Meanwhile, on the personal level in 1987, my father at age 67 was dying of mesothelioma — cancer of the outer lining of his lungs. Mesothelioma is caused by exposure to asbestos. About twice a year, he had received deliveries of pipes, wrapped in asbestos, for his water well drilling business.

Once or twice a month, I took the fifty minute flight from Albany Airport to MacArthur Airport in Islip, Long Island, over an hour away from my parents' home in Amagansett. Each visit I would spend three or four days there. On one of these trips I'd brought along the paperback *When Bad Things Happen to Good People* by Harold S. Kushner, a rabbi. When I finished reading it, both my mother and Aunt Helen (my father's sister) asked me to leave it behind for them to read.

In the store, I couldn't stop talking about my father. I knew I was not unique in experiencing a loved one suffering from cancer, but it made no difference. The words just kept pouring out. It didn't matter whether it was to a very good friend or to a new customer, I couldn't stop. One man when I finally ran down after a lengthy monologue said, "Geez, I just asked, 'How are you?'"

To my relief, my brother moved back to Amagansett to help my mother care for my father. Fortunately, too, my folks had a doctor friend, who revived an almost extinct service: house calls, enabling my father to remain at home instead of having to go into a nursing home or to a hospital.

With the coming move into the larger new space, I sent out invitations to customers and also widely advertised our Open House Celebration Party on Thursday, October 29th. Calling the local paper, I suggested they might want to do a feature about our expansion, but they had a policy that they only covered initial openings and closings. I futilely pointed out an article on a closing was too late to help, while a feature on an expansion might really boost business.

Three authors autographed books from 11:00 a.m. to 1:00 p.m. at our Open House: Larry Hart with his popular Schenectady books, Bill Healy with his beautiful photography book, *The Adirondacks,* and Joanne Seltzer with her eloquent poetry book. Then from 1:00 to 3:00 p.m., two more authors signed books: Joseph F. Girzone with his *Joshua* books and Frances Weaver with *The Girls With the Grandmother Face*s and *Midlife Musings.*

Aside from creating more publicity at the same cost as one author, multiple authors signing books at the same time provided another advantage. If there were time gaps with no customers, the authors enjoyed talking to each other about the book business, sparing me from having to make small talk during those awkward lulls.

In the latter part of November, I received a call about my father. The end was near. I flew to Long Island again, but instead of his death occurring in the next twenty-four hours as expected, he lived several more days. My father had a very strong heart, which would have been a good thing, if he wasn't battling cancer. I was thankful for the conscientious staff coverage during my absence since it was an extremely busy time because of the normal holiday rush as well as customers coming in to check out the expanded store.

When I returned to the Book Nook, the new space appeared to be particularly light and bright. Filled with a variety of carefully chosen books, it came close to resembling the ideal bookstore I had initially dreamed of creating, even if at 900 square feet, it still had only grown from a tiny store category to a small store category.

In the following months, I noticed that for some customers the Book Nook was evolving into more than just a place to buy books. One woman referred to the store as "my sanity stop." She didn't necessarily buy books each time she came, but after she had browsed in her favorite sections: poetry, bestsellers, and "improve your life," and discussed some titles with me, by the time she was ready to leave, her eyes had become a brighter blue and her step a little lighter.

10. Code Purple

What's the code word again? Orange?

AN hour or two into our workday, either Phyllis Friedson, owner of Creations Gift Shop next door, would call me, or I would call her. The first question was always, "Are you busy?" If the person called was waiting on a customer, she'd say abruptly. "Yes, call you back." Click.

Neither of us ever felt offended; customers always took priority.

In between customers, however, we often phoned with any excuse:

- If we needed help with the wording of an ad.
- If we needed to borrow supplies, such as bags or gift wrap.

- If we wanted to show off a new window display (*"If you can spare a moment, run over and take a look."*)
- If we had made a particularly big sale.
- If the morning was getting later, and we hadn't made any sales.

And then, of course, Phyllis listened to my worries about raising two girls, while I heard about her grown children and grandchildren. It became clear to me, motherly concerns didn't suddenly stop when your children grew up, the way I'd always assumed.

In many ways, Phyllis and I didn't have a lot in common. She was more than a decade older than me, and she always dressed as an asset to her store. Among many hand-crafted items, she also sold clothes, jewelry, and accessories. I told myself I didn't have time to be bothered about hair, make-up, and clothing styles. Phyllis was super-organized; I was, let's say, more "flexible." She was not into books, while, after my family, books were my whole life. She was Jewish: I was raised as a Presbyterian.

But we were similar in our love of our families, our sense of humor, and, of course, our pride in our stores.

After the first couple of years in business, my family began tuning me out when I rambled on about the Book Nook, but Phyllis and I found each other's talk about our stores fascinating, no matter how repetitious our stories.

We took turns pulling the same routine.

"Guess what I'm doing?"

"I don't know, what?"

"What does every good retailer do when she's slow?"

"*Of course.* You're ordering more merchandise."

We appreciated the irony. If our stores were busy, we had no time to order; yet if sales were slow, we felt more inventory would create more sales, and often we were tempted to order when we could least afford it.

On slow days we encouraged each other to vacuum, recognizing that once you had the vacuum in the furthest corner with the cord at its utmost length, it was practically guaranteed that a customer would walk in. When we were desperate for business, rolling up the cord when a customer did appear seemed a small chore.

Both our shops could be considered gift shops, but we carefully refrained from competing with each other. Phyllis didn't carry books or calendars. I tried to limit my sidelines to items that were related to books, such as Madeline dolls or Beatrix Potter ceramic animals. When a new customer finished shopping in my store, I'd ask her if she'd been in "that lovely shop next door that carries hand-crafted items." Phyllis in turn would suggest to someone who had picked up a gift in her store that "perhaps a book from the charming store next door would also make a nice gift."

On rare occasions we would report how a customer had made us a little uneasy. Since most of the time we operated our stores by ourselves, we'd feel a lot better if we could call the other for backup. After much discussion, we devised a system involving the code word "purple" to help each other out in such a situation.

If either of us felt the slightest bit uncomfortable with a customer, she was supposed to interrupt the person with an apology. "Excuse me but I just remembered, I have to make a quick call." Then she was to call the other shopkeeper and work the word "purple" into the conversation. I could say, for instance, to Phyllis, "I wanted to let you know your book, *The Color Purple*, is here." Or she could say, "Judy, the *purple* pottery platter you wanted is here."

Then the other person would rush next door, peek in the front window to see if the police needed to be called, or, if the situation didn't look too grim, casually saunter in to lend support.

We also explained the secret code word idea to our employees, who took over for us on our days off, and to Reggie Boehne, manager of Henry's Dry Cleaning, the store in between Phyllis' and mine. We encouraged everyone to call another store for backup if they felt uncomfortable in any situation. Reggie, for example, could say, "Your *purple* dress has been cleaned and is ready."

Although everyone seemed to think it was a very good idea, I began to have reservations about how effective the system would prove in an actual emergency since every other week someone would ask, "What's the code word again? Pink?"

Even so, the plan did make us all feel a little bit more secure. Fortunately, we never received a call testing our security system.

11. TECHNOLOGY: WORTH THE HASSLE

One couple took advantage of the store's new Books in Print program to find and order several older P.G. Wodehouse books. They seemed such a nice couple that I was disappointed when they didn't return to pick up their books despite phone messages and a mailed reminder. The very day that I decided it was a lost cause and put the books out in the Humor Section, the couple entered the store.

"We have a peace offering for you," the wife said, giving me a snapshot of a store with a Book Nook" sign over its front window. Two palm trees were to the right of the store. She said they had been vacationing in Hawaii when they spotted the sign. They both hit their foreheads with the flat of their hands and exclaimed simultaneously, "The Book Nook! We forgot to pick up our books."

THE rapid advancement of the computer for business and personal use occurred during my years at the Book Nook. When I opened the store in 1983, the computer still seemed a novelty, fun to play games with it, but not much help for my small store.

During the first few years, I brought my home computer to the store and purchased an address label program. I began typing in customers' names and addresses. Using clip art for interest. I could print out newsletters or flyers about special sales or upcoming author visits. From today's perspective, they look very amateurish.

In 1988, our main wholesaler, Ingram, offered a Books-in-Print computer program plus a program to check availability of books at their warehouses. Up until that time, I had been relying on their weekly delivery of microfiche for this purpose. The microfiche reader was not ideal. It was very hard to see, and when the weekly delivery came of the new microfiche, the information on it was already at least a week old.

The new programs sounded wonderful, but it was more expensive than the microfiche system. My old computer didn't have enough memory so I would have to buy a new costly computer, and there wasn't spare money lying around.

My husband, Larry, urged me to jump in and get the new program even though it meant buying an expensive new computer. It didn't take much persuading, especially when we went to Sears Business Center and saw their state of the art, beautiful but ultra expensive IBM XT computer, and I found that the payment could be spread out monthly.

The programs turned out to be just as wonderful as I had hoped. What's more, we were the only bookstore in the area for a few years to have this capability of instantly knowing whether a book was in print, or whether it was available at Ingram so that if it was, I could state confidently, "The book will arrive in two days." (In a few years' time Ingram had built a warehouse in Connecticut, and if we placed an order by 11 a.m., the book appeared by the following morning.)

The new programs could also instantly generate lists of titles. For example, if someone asked about French architecture books, I could hand her a list of titles and tell her how quickly they could come in. If a teacher wanted children's books about crocodiles I could hand him *Lyle, Lyle Crocodile* and offer to print him out a list of other titles that could be ordered.

The Books in Print and Ingram's ordering programs ran with very few glitches. Trying to produce camera-ready ads for local newspapers and to produce and send out newsletters, however, I experienced endless frustration. For example, I placed an ad in the *Daily Gazette* bragging about the new Books in Print program (*Challenge us!*) It took me half a day trying to get the spacing right for that 1-inch by 3-inch ad. It did look better than usual, making me feel that the time spent on my day off hadn't been wasted, but there was still a lot of room for improvement for the ad to look truly professional.

Newsletters sent to customers did sell books, but at the time they were very labor-intensive and costly. I wrote them, designed them, and took them to Office Max to make multiple copies. Next I printed out the address labels. Finally (with help from my daughters usually), I folded the newsletters in thirds, stapled them, stuck on the address labels, stuck on the fourth-class stamps, and mailed them. [*In the late 1990s, the ABA (American Booksellers Association) produced a newsletter each month that member bookstores could use and personalize for their stores. By this time, of course, with e-mail becoming prevalent, it could be sent out to customers electronically. It was too late for the Book Nook, however.*]

When I mailed out the newsletter the first time with its computer-generated address labels, my computer showed I had input over 1300 addresses, but this proved to be an inaccurate count. Several people came into the store to show me they had received multiple copies. Aside from the thought of the money wasted, it was very embarrassing. The problem was every time I inserted a name and address into the computer, if there were even a one letter change from the same name or address already in the computer, the program considered it a brand new label.

My store printer refused to work one year during the push to get out a holiday newsletter. It shut down completely when I tried to print out the address labels. Luckily, I had just purchased a new Epson printer for home use. Not too certain it could handle address labels, out of desperation I lugged it to the store anyway. To my amazement, it worked beautifully. In less than twenty minutes, over 1000 labels were printed! I looked upon it as my second technology miracle.

The first, of course, being the Books-in-Print and Ingram's Direct Access Ordering Programs.

12. SURVIVING THE HOLIDAY SEASON

A customer had selected a couple of Hanukkah books for his nieces and was looking over my shoulder as I started to search on my computer for more Hanukkah titles. I pushed a key to obtain direct access on-line service to my major wholesaler, Ingram, to check stock availability of a title he particularly wanted. It would usually have taken about three seconds on my wonderful new program, but this time I could only say after several attempts, "Darn!" and read back to him the message, "Failure to connect. Try again."

He said ruefully. "That's the story of my life actually."

PEOPLE who came into the Book Nook on the supposedly busiest shopping days of the year, the Friday or Saturday after Thanksgiving, were surprised to find it wasn't jammed with customers. While shoppers flocked to the malls to find the heavily advertised bargains on the weekend after Thanksgiving, lack of crowds in smaller stores such as ours on Upper Union Street was typical. Instead, we made our biggest sales in December. In fact, 35% of the Book Nook's sales for the year occurred during that month, with the big push usually coming the last two weeks before the 25th.

From Thanksgiving on, contrary to our usual antipathy toward the white stuff, we merchants on Upper Union Street hoped for snow. Not a big storm, just two to three inches to remind shoppers that the holidays were coming and that the roads might not be that easy to navigate if they procrastinated.

Instead of Black Friday, the Book Nook's biggest day of the year was Christmas Eve. People had checked out their presents and realized they were one or two gifts short. They rushed to the Book Nook to fill the gap. Motivated buyers tried to find quickly *something, anything,* and yes, they definitely wanted their book(s) wrapped.

That's not to say Holiday shoppers didn't come earlier. There were always those *Early Bird Shoppers* who would proudly announce on July 30th or some other ridiculously advanced date, "That's it. I'm through with my Christmas shopping!" I struggled to insert a note of sincerity into my voice as I congratulated them.

In October each year, the Book Nook sponsored a 20% off calendar sale. Customers who liked the 365-day-calendars of Bible verses or Dilbert cartoons or the beautiful Adirondack wall calendars became accustomed to coming in that month to take advantage of the sale and order multiple copies of their favorite calendar for holiday gifts. We also promoted cookbooks each November with a 20% off sale. Incidentally, the best-selling cookbooks were either the healthy ones, such as *The Moosewood Cookbook*, or at the other extreme, cookbooks with the words "Decadent," "Dessert," and/or "Chocolate" in the title.

In December in contrast to the rest of the year, I usually had another person working with me. My staff and I tried to be particularly helpful during this month, hoping to strike a contrast to the mall stores. Often a customer would come in and say, "Whew! I've been to the Mall, and I am so-o-o exhausted." We would suggest they sit down, and we'd bring the books to them. If they had packages from other stores, we'd offer to put them in the back room so they could look at books unencumbered. If they had other shopping on Upper Union Street or wanted to eat lunch nearby, we would offer to keep all their packages until they were ready to pick them up. If we weren't too busy, we would carry older customers' books out to their cars.

Our regular customers in return were very understanding. When we were frantically busy, they would slip me lists of books they wanted, suggesting I call them at home later about availability, or if they had chosen several books that they'd liked wrapped, they said that they would come back later for their packages.

Customers shared their holiday traditions. One woman purchased a bunch of books each December, and explained when we automatically offered to wrap them for her that she didn't need them wrapped. On Christmas Eve, she spread them out under the tree unwrapped and unlabelled among all her large family's other wrapped presents. On Christmas day, everyone waded in and selected the title that appealed to him or her the most. Naturally after the books were read, a lot of swapping occurred.

I generally succeeded in being pleasant to everyone at this time of the year, *except* toward parents who let their small children destroy expensive hardcover picture-books. They really caused me to grind my teeth. Knowing this, before I could snap at a negligent parent, the staff member working with me that day would step in quickly before any damage happened and gently steer the child to the box of worn books and toys we had on hand for just these circumstances.

Even though autograph sessions in December were usually popular, I seldom scheduled them then because customers who weren't interested in the featured author's books stayed away from the store, not just the scheduled two hours, but the whole day, afraid we'd be overrun with customers. (I wished!) Book signings, however, in October and November usually proved to be very successful.

13. HOLIDAY JOURNAL, PART I

B. K. picked out a couple of books for Christmas presents. On the way to the sales counter she spotted Sue Bender's attractive book, PLAIN AND SIMPLE, about lessons learned from the Amish. She leafed through it longingly, sighed, put it down, and said, "No, I can't buy it." She paused and looked at me expectantly. I've always respected when customers say, "No," but I've come to realize if they didn't move away or change the subject, they were hoping to be talked into buying the book.

"It is a lovely book," I said.

"But it's so much money."

"It's better to buy this than wasting money buying junk food at the grocery store. This is something that will last."

"I know." She sighed, still looking at me expectantly.

Searching for something more to say. I finally came up with what seemed a weak reason, but I said it firmly. "You deserve it!"

"You're right! I'm always buying things for my ungrateful kids. I need this. Would you put it on my Visa, please."

"Certainly."

"God! you're good."

It's just that I now recognize when a customer is silently wishing that I give her a reason – sometimes several reasons – to justify buying a book.

10/22/90

I returned last Monday from NEBA (the New England Booksellers' Association Convention). I got carried away writing about it and the interesting books I saw there for my next Book Chat column. The column needs to be drastically cut before I hand it in to the *Niskayuna Journal*.

Store receipts weren't that great last week except for a couple of days. I decided to advertise at least once a week until Christmas. It's costly but necessary.

We have such delightful customers. Mrs. G. called Saturday asking if I'd wrap *Millie's Book* about George and Barbara Bush's dog for her husband to pick up and take to a friend in the hospital. They're both in their nineties and until last winter looked like a lively pair of sixty-year- olds. She's been in the hospital and is home now. Her voice is still strong, and she enthusiastically ordered Senator Patrick Moynihan's new book and two copies of *The Road from Coorain* (I keep selling out the store copies) to give to friends. Mr. G., looking very frail, teetered in an hour later, to pick up *Millie*. He's very hard of hearing. I shuddered to think of him still driving.

L.W. came in to pick up a book for Mrs. H, *Royal Sisters*. She asked if she'd paid for it, and I said no, much to her disgust. Yet when I told her Mrs. H could mail me the check, she insisted on paying for her.

I showed L.W. the beautiful poster from Reeve Lindbergh's children's picture book, *Johnny Appleseed*, which is illustrated by Will Moses, a relative of Grandma Moses. Reeve Lindberg spoke at a NEBA dinner, and she had casually mentioned she was the daughter of Charles and Anne Lindbergh, causing audible gasps from the audience. When I returned, I ordered twenty copies (a lot for me) of her book from Ingram, but with Charles Lindbergh's daughter as the author I am sure it will get lots of publicity, and if I order a smaller number and need to re-order; it might well be out of stock everywhere.

The morning mail brought Mrs. H's check so I will have to reimburse L.W. So many silly tiny details become time-consuming.

I. F. came in and paid $20 toward her lay-away books. She saw two more books and asked me to put them aside until next week when her paycheck comes through. Have other customers like her. I start to show them books they might like, and they'll say, "I'll take them!" I just wish those customers came in more frequently, and I had dozens and dozens more of them.

Skyline Designs called to say freight charges for the counter I had bought from them at NEBA at the special sales price of $200 would be $134! At the show, I had guessed that the freight charges would be about $100, and the rep told me it would probably be a lot less which made me decide to buy it. I mentioned that and the Skyline rep apologized and dropped the freight price to $110. The total price ($310)   still seems expensive for a counter I'm not too certain about. Larry wasn't with me, but he had wanted a Franklin or Storebest wraparound counter. Although he's usually right about these things, I just couldn't see how a wraparound counter would fit in the store space, but I am nervous. I wish he'd been with me to see it before I bought it.

A middle-aged couple came in next. Aside from acknowledging the husband who isn't that into books, I usually spend all the time with the wife. However, I noticed he was eyeing our Civil War books in the window. "Feel free to wade right in there, and look at any book," I said. "Those hardcover books about the generals are a very good buy at only $7.98 each." For the first time, he bought books, one about Sherman and one about Grant.

Unfortunately, I tried to show Mrs. S. a couple of books, but didn't zero in on her interests this time and had to force myself to stop. She was obviously distracted by other things going on in her life and couldn't concentrate on books that day. Sometimes people find looking at books very soothing, but not always.

Two other younger couples came into the store next. I didn't know them, and they announced in a belligerent and challenging tone that they were just looking "*if-that's-all-right!*" Each of the four had to announce that same comment to me in the same challenging tone.

New customers are often afraid that unless they are very firm, I would be piling books up in their arms and snatching the money out of their wallets to pay for them. I am very careful to let this type of customer shop on their own. Often they feel comfortable enough by their third or fourth visit to demand when they enter the store, "Judy, show me a good book."

14. HOLIDAY JOURNAL, PART II

For many years about mid-November, a woman would call, list the ages of her five grandchildren, and ask me to pick out a bunch of books they might like. Her husband would come in and cart them back to his invalid wife. She would look them over at her leisure. A couple of days later, he would return the ones she didn't want and write a check for the ones she wanted to keep.

10/29/90

WITH the holiday season approaching, I won't have too many more Mondays off.

The new counter came mid-week. It's much better than I remembered. Placed perpendicular to the old counter, it fits snugly in the empty space at the pay station. Slanted shelves display books on the customer side and a couple of shelves are for storage on the staff side. It will be a perfect second counter when I have an employee working with me. Even with only one person working in the store, it's also another place for people to park books they are thinking about buying while they continue to browse.

Phyllis came over from Creations when the counter arrived and admired it, and Larry stopped in on his way home from work and raved about it, forgetting all about his preference for a wrap-around counter. Both think it is an excellent buy.

Phew!

D.M. came in Thursday to pick up a $2.95 paperback order. She wanted two more picture-books for gifts. She also took *Road from Coorain* on my recommendation. Then, as I was adding up, she pulled *Mrs. Sharp's Traditions*, a $60 book from the wall unit and another $40 book. Barely glancing at them, she had reached $200 by the time she'd left. She said she's told a lot of her literary friends in Lake George about the Book Nook, that we have the same eclectic mix as Northshire Bookstore in Manchester, Vermont, only it's quieter, and I might add (but didn't), a heck of a lot smaller with a lot fewer books and a lot fewer customers. It would be wonderful to be a destination store like Northshire. I love that store, but if we were as large as Northshire, I'd be a manager of a large number of employees, not an active participant in every area of bookselling the way I am now. I would miss that.

From the beginning, people have often mentioned to me what a wonderful store Northshire Bookstore is.

I agree, and Larry and I visit there at least twice a year, but for a long time I resented these comments, thinking they meant, "Now there's a really great bookstore, especially compared to the tiny Book Nook." Gradually, I've come to realize I've been completely misreading people's intentions. Instead of being insulting to the Book Nook and while not as specific as D.M., they were actually paying the Book Nook a compliment. They meant, "The Book Nook is a delightful store, and it reminds me of another delightful bookstore, Northshire Books." It might be like comparing someone's back yard garden to Brooklyn's Botanical Gardens, but like the gardens, both bookstores are lovely in their own unique way.

About fifteen other people came into the store throughout the day, and their purchases only came to a little more than $200. Then M.M. came in. She hasn't been in for awhile. She told me she needs a new car and can't buy books. I keep hoping she'd get that purchase behind her so she'd feel free to spend money again, but maybe she's decided there's still life in her car after all. Despite saying she only wanted to order just one book, she heard me describing Larry Hart's new book to the customer before her, and she decided she wanted that one and all his others as well.

A furious man barged in about 3:30 Saturday. "You said my book on First Publishing would be here by the end of the week!"

"Yes," I agreed. "I had promised that, and it came in, and I left you a phone message yesterday morning." As I took his money, he complained about the dry cleaning shop next door closing at noon on Saturdays. He had a function to go to that evening and needed the suit he had left for dry cleaning. He ranted on and on. As he made his way down the aisle and out the door, he was still mumbling about it to himself. Suddenly, it must have hit him that the Book Nook had come through for him, because he turned back and shouted, "Thanks for the book. Really, thank you so much for the book. I appreciate your getting me the book so quickly. Thanks. Thanks. Thanks."

11/5/90

Larry's so sweet. He cleaned up most of my storeroom junk on Saturday. I really hadn't wanted him to do it because I worried I wouldn't be able to find anything again. Now that it's done and so much neater, it's easier to find things, or at least not harder. I'm so relieved since I couldn't begin to think how I was going to get it cleaned up in time for Larry Hart's visit.

More people than usual mentioned my column in the Journal last week. Not sure if it's because it's on the back page and easier to spot than usual or my column about NEBA (New England Bookseller's Association Convention) was interesting.

My inventory looks good, especially children's books.

A small stuffed toy, a lamb, as in *Mary had a Little Lamb*, which opens to a small cloth book came in with Ingram's orders. I thought it was over-priced at $9.95, but sold four of the ten copies on Saturday, the first day I put them out. I think *You in a Book* should be effective, too, *if* I ever get samples. The producers of this personalized book (composed of pictures and details of the purchaser's favorite child) swear I will. [*People loved the concept of this personalized book, but the estimates of its publication times were unreliable, and I had to discontinue offering it.*]

Saturday, four sisters returned to look at their old house on Lexington Ave., and stopped in to see the Book Nook. Two grabbed *Mrs. Sharp's Traditions* and played tug-of-war with it for about five minutes. I was sure it would tear in two. A miracle it wasn't destroyed. Even when one sister won, the other kept saying, "I will not let you spend all that money on me."

Lots of orders were placed early in the week; not many later in the week. Mrs. G. came in to pick up her order of Pat Moynihan's book and *The Road from Coorain*. She raved about about an earlier order she had placed, *Worms Eat my Garbage,* and ordered eight more copies to give as Christmas gifts to her equally (I hope) enthusiastic friends.

11/12/90

Wednesday night I wrote most of my Book Chat column for *The Niskayuna Journal* about Larry Hart's books. I hope that the newspaper will give the column a prominent space so readers notice that Hart will be autographing his books next week at the Book Nook.

My main goal this last week has been getting the newsletter out, but it has given me many headaches. I took it to the photocopiers early last Tuesday morning.

Larry was away this last weekend for business, and Tricia was away, too, visiting Ginny. It's nice to have some time alone, but bad timing. Over one thousand newsletters to staple, stamp, and stick on labels was not fun to do by myself.

I pushed myself all last week and met my deadline of getting the newsletters ready to mail today, but arrived downtown this afternoon at the post office and rattled the doors several times before I realized it's Veteran's Day; and, of course, it's closed! Bulk mail doesn't open until 10 a.m. tomorrow.

Sue agreed to come in again tomorrow morning so I can mail the newsletters. So important to get it out for Larry Hart's visit next Monday. Embarrassingly, I got carried away with the r's in Hart's first name (Larrry) and left out James Burnside's name entirely as the author of *The Selling of GE*. I wrote a note of apology to Jim on his newsletter, but he is so nice, I imagine, he will just say he is grateful I am promoting his book. Also, there will be a blank space since I had to call the photocopier at Office Max and ask them to Wite-Out a duplicate line. It's either wait for an expert to proofread and never get them ready, or get it done with errors.

Phyllis went to Chicago. She's very upset. Her sister had to have a heart operation although she seems to have come out of it okay. Bad time too for Phyllis to leave her store, Creations, although she fortunately was able to get coverage. I miss her.

Friday, Troy Savings Bank was robbed at 4 p.m. FBI in to see me at 6 p.m. on Saturday. They asked me if I had any African American customers in the preceding afternoon, and if I had seen any suspicious activity on the street. I sit back too far to see any action on the street and, fortunately, although I have a few regular African American customers, none had been in that day. I would have hated for them to have come under an FBI investigation.

15. HOLIDAY JOURNAL, PART III

When Ron, the UPS man flitted in each day bringing between one and eight cartons of books, he never spent more than three minutes, yet we managed to learn quite a bit about each other over the years. I didn't realize quite how much until one hectic day a week before Christmas. He delivered several boxes of books, and then picked up the outgoing packages, including two to my family. As he went out the front door, he suddenly ducked back in and called, "Congratulations on getting your Christmas presents to your brother on time this year."

1/7/91

LARRY HART was late. That made me extremely nervous, especially because on that November 19, 1990 day, we had a big crowd eagerly waiting to meet him and have him sign copies of his new book, *The Darkest Hour,* a historical fiction book about a Union

College graduate from Schenectady fighting in the Civil War.

He *finally* arrived twenty minutes past the time he was due. Apparently, he had almost reached the store when he suddenly remembered I had asked him to bring more copies of his new book "just as back up." I forgave him immediately, considering he'd brought with him one hundred copies, way over what I'd thought we would need, but we were down to the store's last ten by the time he'd appeared.

Our new counter, set perpendicularly to the old counter, worked well. Ann called out continually to people in the line behind the old counter, "I can help people over here." So we moved people right along.

It was a very successful autograph session. The timing was right for holiday presents, and *The Darkest Hour* appealed to Union College people, Civil War buffs, and Schenectady history fans. We also sold quite a few of Hart's earlier books about Schenectady.

Hart liked our Civil War window and on the following Monday he brought in a sword, pictures of Lincoln, and other mementoes to add to it, much improving the display.

December was the same hectic rush it alway is. Seven days a week, twelve hour days.

The manager of Troy Savings Bank asked me mid-December how the store was doing. I hesitated, and she rephrased, "Is it doing the same as last year, worse, or better?" I told her definitely better, but didn't add it should be much more. She said in that case, compared to other merchants on Upper Union Street, I was doing very well. Everyone else was having a horrible year.

Our hours in December were 10:00 to 7:00. Monday through Saturday and Sunday 12:00 to 5:00. Practically every day I was there early anywhere from 7:00 a.m. to 8:00 a.m., and I could have used a lot more time. Larry was not happy with me coming home so late.

I scheduled an extra person to come in only from 10:00 to 2:00 for the first weeks in December and only scheduled a full day of extra help for the week preceding Christmas (Last year it had been a full day for two weeks but I really hadn't needed so much help the first week). As usual people came in waves. There wouldn't be any one in for a half an hour, then seven people lined up at the counter, and the phone would ring, one call after the other.

One Saturday morning, D.M. walked in, and I was disappointed that I couldn't wait on her because I was tied up with a man selecting books for his nephews—like most men buying for boys, he started with Tolkien's books. I realized it didn't matter that I couldn't wait on D.M. because in a matter of minutes she'd purchased $400 worth of books from Tricia who was working with me in the store that day. One of the books she purchased was *You Just Don't Understand* by Deborah Tannen. During a lull, I started to tell Tricia how the book shows each sex interprets things so differently, but she impatiently cut me off telling me she had seen the author on Phil Donohue's Show. *Where is that little girl who used to hang on my every word as if I were imparting the wisdom of the ages?*

Lots of new people in. Some of whom I think will be good future customers. This time of year we also saw many whom Phyllis from the Creations Gift Shop next store labels the "mall crowd," the pushy, impatient variety.

Children's book selections in the store were excellent. I really concentrated on fine editions and received many compliments, and, even better, made many sales. *The Very Busy Cricket* by Eric Carle, was our biggest children's book sale. Reeve Lindbergh's book, *Johnny Appleseed,* sold well, too, just not as many as I thought it would. Fortunately, children's books don't go out of style like most adult bestsellers. The ad in the *Daily Gazette* about the *American Girl* series books drew in many. As for adult books, the *New York Times* best sellers didn't do very well. There was too much competition at cut rate prices elsewhere. Other types such as coffee table books, local history books, self help books, and cookbooks sold fairly well; mysteries always sell.

It was frustrating that the *Daily Gazette* made gift book suggestions but used the national wire services as the source. They did quote one area bookstore owner who gave recommendations, but it was not from a Schenectady bookstore,   but an Albany children's bookstore!

The Book Nook newsletter was very successful. Every single book mentioned in it was requested by someone.

Pat, the President of BPW (Business and Professional Women's Organization), came in one day a week before Christmas, and said their original candidate for the Capital District Enterprising Women Contest Avon was sponsoring, had not qualified. Would I be BPW's nominee instead? The nomination had to be submitted by the following day. Bad timing for me as she knew, but she said if I would answer their questions, she would type it out for me on Avon's form. The actual event would be January 27. I didn't want to turn down any free publicity for the store so that evening I spent three hours figuring out how to answer Avon's extensive questions. Pat retyped my entry on their special form the next day and submitted it. I am not too uptight about it as I know I will only remain a nominee and not be chosen as the main winner. Other candidates have to be making much more money than I am. As one of the nominees, I will still have to make a short speech about my business, but by this time, I've given enough speeches that I am used to it, and know the main focus will be on the winner. I intend to enjoy myself while getting free publicity.

Good to have extra help, not only so customers wouldn't be kept waiting long, but because in the down times staff could dust and stock shelves. While they were doing this, Ida or Gretchen would often talk to me, which was most annoying. Even if I wasn't actively doing something, I needed time to think and assess what needed to be done. What was even more annoying, instead of telling them firmly I needed a quiet time to regroup, I couldn't refrain from chatting back.

16. ABBY NOMINATIONS OUTSELL NEW YORK TIMES BESTSELLER LIST

I.F. called from the doorway, asking about the newly released GONE WITH THE WIND paperback sequel, "Is SCARLETT here?"

"Yes," I replied. "She's here, but unfortunately Rhett left."

"That's because he didn't give a damn." She shot back.

IN January of 1991, the ABA (American Bookseller's Association) announced the ten nominees for the first ABBY award, the titles booksellers across the country "had enjoyed hand-selling the most." I displayed these books on the wall unit over the book cart near my desk, and these ten books outsold *The New York Times* bestsellers many times over, not only when the list came out, but for years afterwards when they weren't so prominently displayed.

Here are the ten nominees, listed alphabetically, which I wrote about at the time in my Book Chat column:

- *Animal Dreams by Barbara Kingsolver (Harper Collins)*

In this novel, Codi Nodine returns to her hometown in Arizona and through dreams, myths, and day to day living is forced to re-examine her childhood and face her fear of commitment. It's excellent, but I enjoyed Kingsolver's earlier novel, *The Bean Trees* more.

- *The Bean Trees by Barbara Kingsolver (Harper Collins)*

Spunky Taylor Greer manages to achieve her two goals: avoiding pregnancy and getting away from rural Kentucky. She heads for Arizona where she reluctantly becomes responsible for a three-year-old Native American girl named Turtle.

- *The Civil War: An Illustrated History, edited by Geoffrey Ward and Ken Burns (Knopf)*

This large volume was the companion book to the very popular PBS series and had the unusual distinction for such an expensive ($50) book of also reaching *The New York Times* bestseller list.

- *Cold, Sassy Tree by Olive A. Burns (Houghton Mufflin)*

Whenever I attempted to explain the plot of this Southern novel to customers, they inevitably chose something else. Several months later, they usually told me they had read the most marvelous book called *Cold,*

Sassy Tree. After a while, I merely handed people the book with the comment, "Here's one you should read." They were hooked if they only glanced at the first page.

- *The Education of Little Tree by Forrest Carter (University of New Mexico Press)*

This true story reflects a Cherokee boy's childhood during the 1930's and was first published in 1977, returning to print in 1986. Let's hope it never goes out of print again. It is a wonderful book, humorous and touching, and reveals so much of value in a different culture.

Wait! Wait! Wait!

I wrote the above paragraph for my Book Chat column. However, it turned out this book is not a true story but actually a hoax written by a segregationist and Ku Klux Klan member, Asa Earl Carter! He wrote many speeches for George Wallace supposedly including Wallace's famous line, "Segregation now, Segregation tomorrow, and Segregation forever." When the author's background was discovered, The University of New Mexico Press reissued the book as fiction. I consoled myself that this book could still be worthwhile as long as it was properly labelled as fiction despite the troubling background of the author. After all, some artists have shady reputations but that doesn't detract from the beauty of their art. Keep reading, however, to the end of this chapter to find out the problem with that reasoning.

- *Fried Green Tomatoes at the Whistle Stop Cafe by Fannie Flagg (Random House)*

Anyone who remembered Fannie Flagg's imitations of Ladybird Johnson and her family were surprised to find she'd also written a funny, memorable novel. Readers follow several fascinating characters starting with Mrs. Threadgoode in the nursing home; Evelyn, who is going through a middle-age depression; and best of all, Ruth and Idgie, who run a small restaurant in Whistle Stop, Alabama.

- *Remains of the Day by Kazuo Ishiguro (Knopf)*

In this thought-provoking novel, the epitome of the English butler (think Jeeves, Hudson, and Mr. Belvedere, but stuffier) examines the meaning of his life of service to his master, an old-style gentleman, during a road trip. Did he miss out on too much by trying to be absolutely the best at his job, and how should he handle the rest of his life? The author develops these questions and others with poignancy and subtlety.

- *The Road From Coorain by Jill Ker Conway (Knopf)*

A customer bought this book by a former Smith college president who describes her younger years growing up in Australia. My customer planned to send the book to friends in Australia since she said they had never heard of it. That bore out the author's contention that the most respected literature in Australia is by English authors, and that native authors receive very little recognition. Beautifully written, the book is fascinating on different levels: as a description of life on an isolated sheep farm; as a personal study of conflict between duty to others and to one's own destiny; as an indictment of the macho mentality in Australia; and as a testament to the over-reliance of holding up English culture as a model.

- *The Shell Seekers by Rosamunde Pilcher (St. Martin's)*

"There must be some women left in the United States at least in the 1990s who hadn't read this, "nice" is the word I heard most frequently, novel, but I hadn't met them. Part of the appeal was the attractive flowered cover, which also extended to the inside of the cover on the hardcover edition. Once they had the book in their hands, customer after customer said, "I don't know what it is, but this book just appeals to me so much." After *The Shell Seekers* many romance novels developed more attractive feminine covers, often adorned with flowers.

- *When I am an Old Woman I Shall Wear Purple, edited by Sandra K. Martz (Paper Maiche Press)*

This anthology of short stories and poetry features older women. It shows an arresting color picture of a very wrinkled woman on the cover with many more black and white pictures of elderly women throughout the book. Middle-aged women bought this book. Perhaps we liked the idea of the older woman breaking out and doing what she wants with her life, as well as the idea that wrinkled appearances didn't matter. Based on the extreme reaction of elderly customers, however, I warned people not to buy this book to give to women in their seventies or older; that they literally wrinkled their noses in disgust at the pictures.

[*Now that I am in my eighties myself, I understand why those former older customers hated those pictures. The title poem still seems relevant as an ideal for senior women, but the ancient witch-like crone on the cover does not reflect the ideal appearance of an older women. However, in the fourth 2010 edition of WHEN I AM AN OLD WOMAN, I SHALL WEAR PURPLE, the older woman on the cover has changed to someone who could be in her eighties or beyond but is much less wrinkled and crone-like, someone we would be pleased to look like.*]

In my column, I listed three reasons why I voted for *When I am an Old Woman* to be the ABBY winnner:

1. Joanne Seltzer, a local resident, had eight poems in it (under the heading "Finding a Place for Mother.")
2. It was fun to recommend (just not to really old people) since people would buy one copy and return for several more to give to friends.

3. It would have been exciting to see this little California based publisher with exactly ten books listed in Books in Print at the time, win against mega-corporation style publishing houses.

Other booksellers, however, decided that *The Education of Little Tree* should be the winner. Obviously, I wasn't the only one moved by the book, but it faced enormous controversy as I described earlier, following the announcement.

What's more my theory that the book could stand on its own was shot down by the Cherokee Nation who objected to the book for at least two reasons:

1. It claimed the book characters were stereotyped, not typical of real people.
2. The book got many of the Cherokee Nation's customs wrong.

What a shame.

17. Disturbing Books

Based on my memory of customers reporting which books had terrorized them the most, I helped a man pick out horror and occult paperbacks for his eighteen-year-old daughter. While he was paying, I glanced again at the gruesome covers, shuddered, and commented, "She doesn't want to be alone when she reads these."

"Oh, she's alone all right," he said. "She's in prison."

IN contrast to the preceding chapter about books that independent booksellers had enjoyed hand-selling the most, this chapter describes three books that I had found the most unsettling during the nineteen years of the Book Nook's existence. The following books, two non-fiction and one novel, were published within three years of each other, 1988 - 1991.

- *The Satanic Verses by Salman Rushdie*

When in February 1989, the Ayatollah Khomeini called for the assassination of Salman Rushdie for writing *The Satanic Verses* — which had a section Muslims considered very blasphemous — the novel quickly became a bestseller. If the death threat hadn't been made, the author undoubtedly would have remained a respected, but only a mid-list author. Despite *The Satanic Verses'* positive reviews, only a few of the Book Nook's customers were drawn to its "magical realism" style.

Yet after the death threat, customers rushed in to buy *The Satanic Verses*, determined to show that the Ayatollah couldn't dictate what authors could write. They also wanted to support an independent bookstore. Because of threats in some of their stores to employees, as well as a few damaged front windows, most chain bookstores pulled *The Satanic Verses* from their shelves. An employee of the local Waldenbook's told me that she had two men warn her, "Walden's better not carry that book."

I displayed the book in my front window, which in hindsight was more foolishness than bravery. My husband and I argued about it. Because of his persistence, I took it out of the front window. I didn't place it in the back room, however, as he had wanted, but kept it on the bestseller display in the store. I told each of my staff who substituted for me on Mondays, my day off, that if they felt uncomfortable with the book in the store to feel free to remove it to the back room. When I returned on Tuesdays, it was always still on the bestseller shelf.

- *From Cradle to Grave: The Short Lives and Strange Deaths of Mary Beth Tinning's Nine Children* by Joyce Egginton

Not a fan of true crime books myself, I've never understood why so many people seem fascinated by this type of book, but the genre certainly is popular. Look at the book, *Midnight in the Garden of Good and Evil* by John Berendt, published in 1994 about a murder in Savannah, Georgia. The book remained 242 weeks on The New York Times bestseller list, a record that still stands.

However, because the crimes in *From Cradle to Grave* occurred locally in Schenectady (1972 - 1985), I did read the book from cover to cover. I found it compelling, but sickening.

From Cradle to Grave chronicles the nine deaths of Marybeth Tinning's small children. The first death was probably caused by a legitimate congenital disorder. The mother was showered with sympathy and attention. With each subsequent death, suspicion turned more and more toward Marybeth. It seems incredible that she wasn't arrested, if not by the second death, surely by the time of the fifth one, let alone the eighth!

Yet, the book shows the dilemma for authorities. The autopsies were inconclusive. Also, there had been much publicity at the time about crib deaths and false accusations of innocent, grief-stricken mothers. *Finally, however, after thirteen years and eight innocent children's deaths, including an adopted child, Marybeth Tinning was arrested, tried, and found guilty.*

When the book was first published in 1989, alerted by all the publicity, many Schenectadians—I assume neighbors, people in the health field, and in positions of authority—rushed to the Book Nook to check out the book. Most weren't interested in buying it, or even reading it. No, their main interest was making sure they weren't mentioned in the book. They'd flip through the book desperately, discover that it had an index, and then run their fingers down the columns to look for their name. If their name was listed, they'd reluctantly buy the book. If their name wasn't in the index, they'd breathe a huge sigh of relief, and leave without buying the book.

- *Final Exit: The Practicality of Self-Deliverance and Assisted Suicide for the Dying by Derek Humphry*

When *Final Exit* was first published in 1991, many people, including myself, were anxious to read it. Suicide wasn't something we wanted to do, but it did

seem practical to have a method on hand in case we—
or someone we loved—might ever be in unbearable
pain or have contacted a disease that would turn us into
a zombie. We wanted to know a painless, simple way to
slip out of life in a worst case scenario. When I read the
book, however, I saw that unless you had the assistance
of a doctor, or access to certain types of pills, release
from life did not look that simple. Suffocation by the
plastic bag method was also presented as an effective
method, as well as a backup plan to using pills.

Three people told me, however, that a desperate
family member had asked them to end their lives of
unbearable pain with the plastic bag method, but all
three reported that they were unsuccessful. The instinct
to breathe was too strong, and they each found they
couldn't carry through their loved one's request.
Looking back, I find it incredible that these customers
had shared something so personal, not to mention so
illegal, with me.

When I saw one customer, a pharmacist in one of
the chain drugstores, who often came in to browse on
his lunch break, looking through the book, I asked him
if there were some ordinary ingredients you could mix
together that would do the job. I didn't really hold out
much hope he'd tell me if there were.

He smiled and said that just before his son-in-law
married his daughter, he took him aside. He warned
him, if he didn't treat his daughter decently that he

knew how to mix ingredients that would instantly kill a person. What's more, no one would ever detect that it wasn't a natural heart attack.

I never determined whether this was a bluff on his part or a serous threat, but it did prevent me from further quizzing him about the ingredients for a deadly cocktail.

18. CHILDREN'S SPECIALTY

A young boy came into the store with his mother to buy the latest Goosebumps Series Book.

His mother spotted the cassette of Barbara Bush's book and picked it up.

"I've always liked Barbara." I remarked.

"Yes," agreed the boy eagerly, "didn't she make the flag or something?"

WITHIN the first few years of its opening, children's books developed into a major specialty of the Book Nook. Correspondingly, there was an explosion nationally of the publication of children's books.

Jim Trelease's *Read-Aloud Handbook*, published in 1982, the year before the Book Nook opened, influenced much of the increased emphasis on the importance of reading for children. Grade school teachers read aloud to children, plus designated time for silent reading. In addition to the school libraries, teachers began filling bookcases with their own books right in their classroom.

In my talks to parents, I often started with a mention of the *Read-Aloud Handbook*. The points, I noticed people jotting down were:

1. Don't stop reading aloud to children when they reach school age. Continue on.
2. Read aloud every night at bedtime. Not as a reward or punishment. The choice is going to be going to bed without reading or reading.
3. It's very important that fathers should read to children as well as mothers. Reading shouldn't be just seen as something only women do.
4. The recommendation in the book to turn off the television altogether seemed unrealistic to me, but I suggested having just one day a week with no television on. It didn't have to be an all or nothing approach.

I also remarked that in my childhood, girls would read books about boys—sometimes out of desperation since aside from Nancy Drew and Cherry Ames, there were very few books then about girls—but boys didn't read books about girls. I had observed that now eight-to-twelve- year-old boys would often go by a book in my store with a girl as the main character, tap it, and comment to me, "Great book!" These were not books where the girls just sat around discussing their feelings, of course, but books where there was plenty of action, such as *Number the Stars* by Lois Lowry or, especially, *The Adventures of Charlotte Doyle* by Avi.

In contrast, very few grandmothers accepted this idea of boys liking girls' books, however. They preferred to play it safe with books with boys as the main character, and I had no problem finding "unputdownable" books for them with boys as the hero such as *Hatchet* by Gary Paulson or *Maniac McGee* by Jerry Spinelli.

It was also no trouble for me to keep up with children's literature since these books were such fun quick reads and usually well-written. Of course, every year I read the Newbery Medal Winner and the Runner ups, chosen by the American Library Association. Every time a teacher or school librarian visited the store, we swapped the titles of our newest discoveries.

If school librarians had a set amount of money to buy books for a Book Fair or a special project such as Ten Books in a Bag for mothers of preschoolers to borrow, they sometimes asked me to choose the books for them. I eagerly accepted since it saved the librarian's time, and I loved selecting books.

So many parents and grandparents had asked me if I felt Judy Blume books were suitable for children that I decided to read, or in some cases re-read, all her published books at the time (fifteen). I wrote a handout with a synopsis of each, giving my opinion. Seven of her books for young children contained nothing anyone should find objectionable. *Tales of a Fourth Grade Nothing* and its sequel, *Superfudge*, were hilarious.

Surprisingly (surprisingly, if you listened to her detractors, or, like me were shocked by her adult books – while not being able to put them down – most of Judy Blume's books for older children presented a clear-cut moral. She tackled in a fresh, realistic way, many problems faclng children, including: sibling rivalry, physical changes, peer pressure, racial prejudice, handicaps, divorce of parents, and death.

The one Judy Blume young person's book that I had problems with was *Forever* where the heroine had sexual relations with a boy. "However," I wrote, "in this modern age, many people may not agree with my disapproval. The heroine is almost eighteen, takes full responsibility for birth control and feels a strong commitment to the boy." I also cautioned that while I found *Then Again Maybe I Won't* harmless, three mothers whose opinions I respected didn't approve of the book.

I wasn't fond of the very popular Goosebumps Series, even though they flew off the shelves. It wasn't the occult to which I objected, but the use of it. In the closing pages of a couple of the books that I had read, the main child character used it to make a nasty child character vanish. I felt alone in my objection, however, since parents, teachers, and librarians to whom I expressed my misgivings all stated they thought I was overreacting. *"At least it gets them reading."* I felt vindicated, when I read an article by Stephen King, the king of occult books for adults, stating he thought the Goosebumps Series was inappropriate for children. I did urge parents to read the books so at least they could discuss what was in them with their offspring.

One of my favorite books from childhood was *Anne of Green Gables*. For the first few years, at the Book Nook, I pushed the book but had few takers. After the tv series came out, however, it became very popular.

During the 1980s and 1990s publishers produced many beautiful picture books by such outstanding artists as the following: Jan Brett, Eric Carle, Cheng-Khee Chee, Kay Chorao, Tomie DePaola, Susan Jeffers, Thomas Locker, William Moses, Chris Van Allsburg, and Ed Young

I especially enjoyed showing customers the picture book, I *Wish I were a Butterfly* by James Howe with its lovely illustrations by Ed Young. A cricket kept wishing he were practically any other creature than himself throughout the book. On the last page a butterfly flies by and says, "What lovely music, I wish I were a cricket."

A fifth grader, who wrote to James Howe as part of a class project, received a letter back from the author mentioning that he had gone to school in the same town, Niskayuna, as the letter writer. Niskayuna is part of Schenectady County. As a result, Howe came to Hillside Elementary School to interact with the children, including the proud youngster who had originally written to him. He signed several copies of his books as a fund-raising project for the school. After the ensuing publicity, helped by one of my Book Chat columns featuring him, I sold many copies of his books, especially the popular *Bunnicular* series for eight-to-ten-year-olds, which was a perfect read aloud, too, for younger children. Educators readily identified with Howe's picture book, *The Day the Teacher Went Bananas*, illustrated by Lilian Hoban.

In 1985, the Book Nook Contest for children to make book character puppets resulted in only seven children participating. Three years later in 1988, the Book Nook sponsored a Poetry and Drawing Contest, connected to Arnold Lobel's *Book of Pigericks* (One of the limericks in the book involves a pig from Schenectady.) By this time I was a much better promoter, and 780 children participated from 46 classrooms! A few years later in 1993, our *The Tale of Mr. McGregor* Contest — actually *The Tale of Peter Rabbit* written from the gardener's point of view — provided fun for the 460 participants and for the many readers of their hilarious efforts, which I posted in the store. Customers and I would quote the funniest lines back and forth to each other. *"Peter's father didn't*

get baked in Mrs. McGregor's pie. Instead, Peter's father had
run away with a younger bunny."

Simultaneously with the McGregor Contest, our daughter, Tricia, won second place for a window she designed for the store in a national Viking Penguin Bookstore Contest to celebrate the 100th anniversary of the publication of *The Tale of Peter Rabbit.*

One year on a Saturday afternoon, Literacy Volunteers sponsored a Read Aloud Event at the Book Nook. Local TV and radio commentators would read aloud to children in one of our two front windows. Literacy Volunteers provided a couple of rocking chairs; I provided the books. My recall of the occasion is hazy. I only remember TV news commentator, Ernie Tetrault—with a sixty-year background in radio and TV—reading to delighted children. Literacy Volunteers had suggested using some customers, too, to read in the other window. Laura Michelson eagerly agreed and talked my husband into alternating reading aloud with her. Both Laura and Larry remember how much they enjoyed the Read Aloud Event.

The Harry Potter books—first coming out in the United States in 1998 were a phenomenon just in sheer numbers sold. According to Wikipedia, the first book, *Harry Potter and the Sorcerer's Stone,* sold 50,000 in 1998; the second in the series sold 250,000 copies in 1999, and the third sold 500,000 in the year 2000. [*The popularity of these books weren't a passing phenomenon. By 2018, over 500 million in the series had been sold!]*

Hype increased with each successive book in the series: giveaways, contests, a secret language, games, pajama parties in bookstores and schools. Booksellers were on their honor not to sell new releases in the series a second before the given day! I began to feel as if we'd be flung into prison if we violated this order from the American publisher. Children, of course, went along with the razzle dazzle. They *loved* Harry Potter, they told me excitedly. It would take a brave child to buck the trend. It would be almost as shocking as a child declaring she didn't like Santa Claus. But I met that child. She was eagerly gathering some paperbacks to buy, and her mother thrust the latest Harry Potter hardcover at her. "Here. You know everybody loves them."

The eight-year-old girl stuck out her prominent chin and announced firmly, "I know everybody loves them, but I don't happen to be one of them. *I-don't-like-Harry-Potter.*"

I'd love to meet that child today as an adult.

19. COMPETITION SEEMS GREAT UNTIL MY STORE SUFFERS, PART I

(Part of an e-mail to my Mother)

I was checking out the new Borders in Colonie, less than a half-hour away. Of course, I noted down some great books to carry in the Book Nook that will probably sell better in our store than Borders since they won't be buried among so many books. As I was going down the escalator, I spotted one of my good customers on the adjacent up escalator, and I said, "Hello" to him. He jumped, turned red, and looked as if he were a fifth grader caught copying another student's homework. "How embarrassing," he said.

I do hope he returns to the Book Nook soon so I can reassure him that I can understand how a book-lover can't resist visiting a vast selection of books. But, oh, I wish these mega bookstores weren't coming closer.

ONE weekend in mid-September 1992, I drove up and back on my own through the beautiful

Adirondack Lake Country to confirm that our younger daughter was settling in as a Freshman at St. Lawrence University.

Back in the store on Tuesday, refreshed and energized from the trip, I was checking to see what books had been sold during my absence, when the phone rang. It was Phyllis, the owner of Creations, the gift shop next door. She gently told me the grim news. Another bookstore—a children's one—was opening just three blocks away on Upper Union Street!

Needless to say, I was stunned and knew immediately it could spell disaster. Phyllis, while trying to come up with positive suggestions didn't say, "Don't worry." She understood the precarious nature of retailing locally.

Schenectady was a depressed city at the time, due to its biggest employer, General Electric Company, cutting thousands of jobs. When we first moved to the area in 1977 there were over 20,000 employees of GE here. Just fifteen years later, there were less than 5000.

Practically, everybody else tried to reassure me. "You don't need to worry. You've been in business for years [nine actually] and are established, after all." They also commented that the "new store won't be able to make it just selling children's books. You sell to both children and adults."

They meant well, but they didn't understand.

Most people—except for the actual merchants on the street, who usually only voiced how slow business was to each other—thought that the Upper Union Street Area was very prosperous, but it was a false perception.

As for the Book Nook, like most independent bookstores across the country, it wasn't making that much money. Half our sales came from children's books. These books actually were more profitable than the adult ones since they always seemed to stay in fashion. Adult bestsellers had a very short shelf life.

As it got closer and closer to the new store's grand opening on Halloween, the news got worse and worse, and I became more and more jealous. The owner of the new store's business background had been in the publishing business, while mine hadn't been remotely related to the book business. Worst of all, she—I seldom thought of the owner by name, just SHE—must have had several times the opening capital than I had to work with. The new store's fresh inventory already contained more books than I had built up in my children's section after nine years. She also started right away with a full-time employee. It had taken me a whole year just to be able to afford to pay to have someone fill in one day a week allowing me to have a second day a week off, instead of just Sunday when the Book Nook was closed.

As for bookshelves, Cornerstone's were top quality wood ones, while the Book Nook's although wood, had a definite cheaper home-made touch about them. It was only gradually that we had added more professional-looking cases in the center of the store. The most expensive bookcase that I had just acquired was my pride and joy, coming from a place called Skyline Designs.

Dropping in to see the new store on its opening day after I had closed mine for the night, I managed to unclench my jaw just enough to compliment the owner on its lovely appearance. I later griped to my husband that every single one of Cornerstone's many bookcases were Skyline Design, which she told me the owner had delivered himself to her from New Hampshire. Larry asked me if I told her, "Yes, I recognize the make, we have *one.*"

I also vented my frustration about the new store and owner to my mother over the phone, moaning, "And what's more, she's very nice, dammit!"

"What did you say?" my mother asked in an incredulous tone.

She's very nice, *darn it*?"

Mom quickly set me straight. "She's pleasant, if you say so, but, she's *not* nice. Nice people don't open up a bookstore just down the street from my daughter's store." In hindsight, I wished I hadn't been so "nice" myself to the owner of the new bookstore and expressed strongly to her that she obviously would drastically damage my business, plus she hadn't done her own store any favors either by opening so close to me.

To those who weren't familiar with the Book Nook, Cornerstone's staff was automatically considered to be the expert in children's books. Unless they had very strong ties to my store, people looking for juvenile books naturally headed to a children's bookstore instead of a general one.

A representative of an Albany educator's group asked me to make a speech about children's books (which I had been accustomed to giving to parent and teacher organizations) only to renege when she realized I owned "just a general bookstore." She had confused the Book Nook with the children's bookstore on the same street.

People stopped in asking for directions to the new store which I would give them, but I would also mention we had a fine selection of children's books that they might want to check out, too. Most of these people had such a pre-conceived notion that a specialty children's bookstore was the only place to look for children's books that they didn't even spare a glance at my books, really inconceivable to me when they were only five feet away!

My one consolation was that personnel from the new bookstore, Cornerstone, were harassed by questions as well. Loyal customers of the Book Nook reported that when they visited the other store, they demanded, "What on earth possessed you to open so close to another bookstore, especially since the Book

Nook already has such a fine selection of children's books?"

When asked my opinion, I could only speculate that perhaps the owner naively though we would surrender our children's book business and concentrate solely on adult books.

I did consider it — for about a minute — but with my love of children's books, my relationship with teachers and school librarians, and the substantial knowledge I had acquired, I wasn't about to abandon my nine years of building the children's book department without a fight.

20. Competition Seems Great Until My Store Suffers, Part II

(In an e-mail to my mother)

I received our first cash register for the store this week. It also included updating our ordering program software and books in print program from Ingram. The new cash register program records titles sold by category so I can see what sells daily, weekly, or monthly. I didn't get the inventory part of the software yet.

As you know, we've gone over ten years without a cash register. I really don't think most customers have noticed its absence — or cared if they did. Only one customer, L. W. has ever complained about it. She's very supportive otherwise, but for over ten years *every* time I've added up her books — very quickly on the calculator, I might mention — she has remarked, "You need a cash register." So naturally, I couldn't wait to show her the latest purchase.

"Do you see we have a cash register?" I asked.

"What?"

"We finally have a cash register." I said pointing to it.

"Oh, yes," she said vaguely. "I need to order a book."
It's not good business practice to scream at a customer.

I N October 1992, with the opening of a children's bookstore, Cornerstone, just three short blocks away from the Book Nook, I had two options: (1) Surrender the children's books as a specialty and concentrate solely on adult books, or (2) fight back."
I chose option number two.

I battled back and battled back hard.

The week before Cornerstone opened, my husband put up a red banner with white lettering between our front posts outside, announcing :

VISIT OUR CHILDREN'S CORNER

Its $40 cost repaid us several times over since it lasted for the ten more years we stayed in business. Several times a month people came in asking to see "the children's corner."

Cornerstone's first day was Halloween, 1992. I gave a discount off purchases that day for any adult or child who could say successfully the tongue-twister, *Which Witch Whistled?*

The Book Nook ran many children's book sales. In fact, the first December that the new bookstore opened, we held a holiday sale of 25% off all children's books.

I immediately gave teachers a generous year-round discount on children's books.

In the spring of 1993, the Book Nook ran *The Tale of Mr. McGregor* Contest for fourth and fifth graders, resulting in 480 entrants.

We continued to have autograph sessions with children's authors including C.S. Adler, Jennifer Armstrong, Daniel Hayes, Lucinda Landon, Mary Elise Monsell, Karen Pandell, Jack Reber, and Ellen Senisi.

Because of time pressures, I might have formerly turned down some invitations to talk about children's books, but now I accepted all invitations.

I continued to position the Book Nook as a family bookstore. *Books for the whole family.*

During the next couple of years, we did retain a fair amount of business in children's books with our exceptionally large number of loyal patrons. Several of my customers flatly refused to "set foot in that new store." Several others checked it out from curiosity but loyally reported back that they didn't like the selection of books or that the help was too harsh with children looking at the books. I was both touched and amused. I felt Cornerstone's selection was top notch and could sympathize with not wanting expensive books ruined by careless or messy little fingers. Thanks to Sue, one of my employees, we could steer very young children whose parents weren't watching them carefully enough, to a box of used books and toys she had brought in for this purpose.

There was no getting around it, however. Although we kept a substantial part of our children's book customers, a portion was siphoned off to Cornerstone, and we weren't picking up any new customers.

Meanwhile, like other independent bookstores, we were hit in 1993 with Barnes and Noble, and a few months later with Borders putting up their superstores in Colonie, both less than a half hour away.

In 1994, Media Play, with very deep book discounts, opened their doors in time for the Christmas season. It was even closer, at the Mohawk Commons, just a five-minute drive away.

While still busy, 1994's December was not the financial bonanza it usually was.

The owner of Cornerstone stopped in after the holidays to ask how we did. She griped how Media Play had hurt her sales. It was my cue to say how Cornerstone had hurt ours even worse than Media Play, but *Mrs. Non-Confrontational* couldn't do it. Cornerstone's owner noticed a second computer, and the new cash register with our wholesaler's updated ordering system, making it even easier for us to determine how quickly we could order books. She mistakenly thought we had a new computerized inventory system, which really seemed to impress her — as well as depress her. I didn't correct her misconception, just saying it was an Ingram update.

I faltered on through the winter, but in the spring of 1995, I began facing the reality that there was no way to continue the store. Not only had the Book Nook stopped making money; it was losing money.

With a shrinking tax base and rising real estate taxes in Schenectady, it might not be that easy to attract a buyer for the building.

I stayed awake nights not wanting to face reality.

Then our upstairs tenant notified me he was leaving. Another blow, but it allowed me to postpone making the decision to put the building up for sale until we found new tenants. Income from a rented apartment rather than a vacant unit would make the building look much more attractive to a buyer.

Meanwhile, trying to hold on to what little business we had, I strived to put on a cheerful face in the store to customers.

It was at this depressing stage, sometime in late May, a fellow shopkeeper alerted me that she had heard that Cornerstone was closing, and the owner was looking to sell the business. "It's more than a rumor," she insisted.

Dare I hope?

I hung on, praying if the owner with her publishing background and her substantial initial investment couldn't make a success of the store, no one else would dare try.

Walking down to the Book Nook on the morning of July1st, I noticed a sign in Cornerstone's window:

FINAL DAY!

Although I felt a huge sense of relief, I was surprised to feel sad for the owner — at least for that one day.

Our sales of children's books picked up immediately. Even if we didn't have a requested children's book on hand, we no longer heard the comment, "Before I order it, I want to check if it's in the other children's bookstore first." That had meant even if Cornerstone didn't have the book, the customer probably would have ordered it there, rather than going through the nuisance of contacting the Book Nook again. Now, with Cornerstone closing, we again captured all customers looking for children's books on Union Street. Our school order business also increased substantially.

In July and August our children's book sales increased 50%. Also, the newness and allure of the superstores seemed to have worn off. Instead of raving about huge inventories, people began talking about the charm of small stores again.

Within a few months the Book Nook's prospects had brightened considerably. I began answering the phone with enthusiasm once more, knowing it would be a customer on the other end, instead of fearing it was a creditor.

People's reaction to the children's bookstore's closing varied widely. Other merchants and friends congratulated me. "Well, you shot away the competition."

I'd reply, "Today Cornerstone; tomorrow Borders."

The public was shocked at the closing since the children's bookstore had looked so successful. There were different speculations as to why the store closed. Few recognized how precarious the independent bookstore business really is.

"*She carried just children's books, not books for the whole family the way you do.*"

Or, "*It had a New York City store atmosphere. They weren't that friendly.*"

Or the old, "Well, *you're so established.*"

Of course, several people who had never been in the Book Nook until Cornerstone's closing had developed a genuine fondness for it and said, "Isn't it a shame that lovely children's bookstore had to close?"

Obviously, I didn't echo their sentiments, but references to Cornerstone weren't nearly as grating as they had been when the store was open.

It's amazing how a significant increase in cash flow increases one's tolerance level.

21. Thank Heavens I Own a Bookstore, Otherwise They'd Cart Me Away

A man purchased Barbara Kraus' CALORIES AND CARBOHYDRATES COUNTER. "It's a surprise gift for a friend," he told me.

"I hope she's a very good friend," I blurted out.

"You might say that; she's my ex-wife."

It took an extreme effort not to make the obvious comment.

ONCE I opened my bookstore, people looked at me a lot more tolerantly than they did in my pre-bookstore days. I was forgiven immediately for forgetting someone's name, hunting frantically for my keys only to find them in the door, or losing my train of thought mid-speech.

This tolerance is extended to writers and college professors, I hear. For some reason people are ready to excuse as lovable foibles the actions of those of us associated with books, which they would consider grounds for calling in the men and women in white coats for those in other professions.

Having fallen on the icy sidewalk and twisted my ankle rushing to work one Saturday, I waited until Sunday — when the store was closed — to go to the Emergency Room at Ellis. By then my ankle had swollen to the size of a cantaloupe.

After a technician took an x-ray, I hobbled back to one of those claustrophobic cubicles and waited. Finally, a doctor pulled back the curtain and entered. "Where does it hurt?" he asked.

A logical question, but I couldn't remember. At that precise moment for the first time in twenty-four hours, my ankle didn't hurt. I could only look at him blankly.

He said impatiently. "The bottom of the foot? The front? At the ankle? All over? Where?"

"Let me walk on it again." I finally said in desperation and with the first step, instead of trying to put the pain out of my mind as I had been doing for the past day, I could tell him immediately. "A band around the whole ankle."

About then he spotted *Piano Lessons* by Noah Adams, which I had hastily stuffed back in my handbag when he'd come in. His eyes lit up. "Do you play the piano?"

I had to tell him. "No, I'm not at all musical."

He looked at me as if to say that confirmed he had an imbecile on his hands. I quickly explained that I owned the Book Nook on Union Street and was reading some books for a talk at a book club.

Since his wife, like almost every other book-loving person I'd met, had always wanted to own a bookstore, his attitude immediately changed.

He plied me with questions about the store and listened avidly to my every word about the joys—the customers and the books—and tribulations—not that profitable.

Fortunately, the emergency room wasn't very busy because it was only after a lengthy discussion that he reluctantly turned to diagnosing my ankle—badly sprained.

Customers were also very understanding. While they might have become furious at mistakes in another type of store, they tolerated a lot from me in the bookstore. For instance:

- If a customer had a ten-dollar bill in her hand, I'd been known to look right past the amount clearly displayed on the cash register and for an $8.60 purchase announce, "That will be $1.40," (having subconsciously figured the change) or

- handed a book order to a customer that was clearly meant for someone else, or

- telephoned a customer to let him know his book was in and called him by the author's name. ("Mr. Steinbeck, your book is in.")

I usually caught myself making these dumb mistakes almost immediately---unfortunately, a split second after the customer did.

Most people generously implied that they thought I was distracted because I was contemplating the themes in the last three Pulitzer Prize novels, or for other equally lofty reasons. However, my mind usually had splintered into a dozen different directions, all of them a far cry from the exalted thoughts my customers had envisioned.

Did I make a note to call Mr. Z. back? Would I be able to reach the Naval Institute Press to check on the availability of a book without being put on hold again and forced to listen to the first two lines of "Anchors Away" repeated endlessly? Did my daughter have more to say on the phone when I cut her off abruptly a few minutes ago when a customer walked in. Had I missed the Gazette's deadline to get my ad in for Thursday? Would I be able to get coverage for this Friday afternoon and Saturday so I could accompany my husband to an out-of-town business dinner? Did I still have time to get out more news releases for an author visit next week? And my customer mentioning her garden reminded me to include in my order list that great gardening book I saw at the florist yesterday. The pictures alone would sell the book.

All very mundane details, but they did tend to clutter up my mind, making me a trifle absent-minded at times.

I also had a problem trying to remember names. Even the names of people whom I saw quite frequently sometimes eluded me, at least temporarily.

Actually, I was better at remembering what people read than their names. The front door would open, and I would think, here comes Anne Somebody or other, who likes Deepak Chopra's works, or I would meet. "What IS her name?" at the Co-op and give a generic "Hi there" greeting, but would be able to inform her that a new book by her favorite author, Sue Grafton, had just come out.

In my pre-bookstore days, people became insulted when I forgot their names, but once I owned the store, they became much more understanding. ("You see so many people during the day.")

There are plenty of solutions, recommended in any of the numerous books about mnemonics on the market. However, I don't trust any of them.

Take the rule of three. You know the theory: use the person's name whom you've just met three times in conversation, and it's yours forever. Most people using this method, however, don't just stop at three. After just a few minutes conversation, you can recognize immediately anyone using this gimmick in any social or business gathering.

"So pleased to meet you, Judy."

"Great day today, isn't it, Judy?"

"Yes, Judy, I did hear it was supposed to rain tonight."

"Yes, Judy, there certainly is a big turnout here."

"Let me see, Judy, my friend said you own a bookstore? Let me ask you, Judy, have you ever heard of the book...?"

And on and on, until I cringe at the sound of my own name. Worse, the same person would come back twenty minutes later and say, "Good to see you again, Janice."

No, this method was far from foolproof.

Then there's the popular association method. Think of a person's most obvious trait or something striking about their appearance, and relate it to their name as a helpful memory aid. It may work with some people, but it proved disastrous for me the very first time I tried it.

I had just met John Bard, and since his most distinguishing feature was his considerable girth, I thought of fat and then "lard" to rhyme with his last name, "Bard."

After a few minutes chatting with him, one of my friends joined us, and I proudly made the introduction in a loud, clear voice. Although I had used the association method,   unfortunately, I omitted a step, which I realized one second after the following words left my mouth: "Carolyn, I'd like you to meet John Lard."

The bookstore excuse didn't work for a blunder this big.

22. Nothing to Do but Sit and Read All Day

Sometimes, even the smartest people — and my mother was one of the sharpest — can be blinded by love for their children. The apartment over the Book Nook was vacant again. I told my mother that a nice young man who worked at Borders Bookstore in Colonie was eager to rent it, but he needed to bring his girlfriend back to approve it first.

He liked the idea of living over an independent bookstore and said it would be fun to work an hour or two in the Book Nook on his days off.

"Do you think that's wise?" my mother asked.

"Why wouldn't it be?"

"Won't he steal all your good ideas for Borders?"

"Mom, I don't quite know how to break this to you, but the Book Nook is not in the same league as Border's."

Unfortunately, the girlfriend didn't like living on a busy street, easing my mother's concern that Border's would turn into a replica of the Book Nook.

A BOUT once a week a customer in the bookstore would comment to me, "It must be wonderful to sit and read all day; I'd love to work here."

No one who has ever said that has ever ended up working at the Book Nook, I might add.

Several people also suggested that the store might provide the perfect non-pressure job for their slightly deficient relative or friend, something to ease them into the real workaday world at a K-Mart or a Walmart.

Granted we usually didn't have long checkout lines, and our customers didn't feel obligated to yell at the help the way they did at the Department of Motor Vehicles—or so I've heard from a customer who worked there. Practically everybody, however, who has worked at the Book Nook admitted that the job was more complicated than it first appeared.

Large stores have their computers set up to simplify cash, check, and charge-taking so that most anyone can do it; and that's all their cashiers do; they have a manager to answer questions. In contrast, for over ten years at the Book Nook, we didn't have a cash register; instead, we added up purchases on a calculator, noting each price down on a sales pad.

In my store, the staff was substituting for the owner, so that they not only took cash, checks, and charges; they answered inquiries that could be about any book ever printed, any out-of-print book, or even a non-existent book since the customer often did not give the correct title. Staff waited on customers; tactfully kept youngsters from destroying books; used the computer to identify books that customers wanted to order and checked availability at our wholesaler. They called publishers if a customer wanted a book not listed at our wholesalers. They sometimes placed orders. They often made recommendations. They also vacuumed, dusted, and straightened shelves, alphabetizing books by author, and did a window display if they had time in between waiting on customers. In short, they did everything I did except pay the bills.

Even when my employees were away from the store, they fielded inquiries about the book business and would often phone in with an order for a friend or an acquaintance. They should have been earning a lot more than I could afford to pay them. However, I did give a hefty employee discount on their book purchases, which was an attractive lure for these book-lovers. They often commented that even with the discount, they spent more money buying books than they earned.

Aside from my day off, they also worked for me other times: the rare occasions I was sick; when I watched our daughter's soccer games; and when we went on vacation. They worked alone in the store most of the time, but joined me for the December holiday season and for author autograph sessions.

I usually didn't have to advertise for help since book-lovers are often eager to work in a bookstore. One time, however, no one had applied recently so I put a sign in the window, and I was flooded with applicants. Usually my interviewing tactics involved casual questions about past work experience and what type of books applicants enjoyed reading. But this time, I made up a questionnaire. One of the questions on it was: "Would it bother you to work for someone who's messy?" When I threw in that question, I didn't expect anyone to answer "Yes." I just wanted to give fair warning about my sloppy habits. However, one young woman did answer this question with a "yes" and went on to explain, "I like to work on surfaces which are clean and uncluttered."

When I told my mother, the Queen of Neat, that an applicant had actually put down "yes" to this leading question, she advised me to "grab this gem immediately." It's all a matter of perspective. On the basis of that one question, I viewed this applicant as not too bright and a potential nag. My mother admired her honesty and saw her as an ideal worker.

Actually, most of my help turned out to be much neater than I was. Thank heavens they were, however, because if there is anything I can't stand, it's someone else's mess.

Any employee who stuck it out longer than two weeks developed a fierce loyalty to the store, They were extremely conscientious and were adept at helping customers without pressuring them. Each one was an asset in a different way.

In an open staff notebook, we wrote notes back and forth to each other. This is one of my notes:

> *"Gretchen, a customer came in today for the sole purpose of thanking you. She is so grateful. She said last Monday, you had recommended C.S. Adler's paperback, EDDIE'S BLUE-WINGED DRAGON for her nine-year-old son, a very reluctant reader. She didn't have much hope, she said, based on past experience, but she had read only half the first page to him before he literally snatched it out of her hands and began reading it himself!"*

Sue, who had been with the store the longest, set the standard for keeping the shelves dusted and the books neatly arranged. Her specialty was mysteries.

Unlike the rest of the staff, Jeanne welcomed learning the computer programs to look up books in print and availability of stock at our wholesalers. She easily figured out how to change the tape on the new cash register when we finally got one. Jeanne also could interpret how to assemble the cardboard "dumps," resembling mini bookcases that publishers sent us as a bonus to contain a multiple single title order. While I would be gazing blankly at the directions, she'd take one look at the flat pieces of cardboard and say, "Well, obviously this piece inserts into this, and this part goes here. . ." She particularly liked the Irish writer, Maeve Binchy's novels.

Ida endeared herself to me early when she came in on a day when she wasn't scheduled and announced she was going to straighten out the disastrous back room and flatly refused to accept any pay for the added time.

Margaret, a former teacher, has an extensive knowledge of picture books. She would produce on her home computer lovely, large graphic paper signs to go in the front window to advertise our monthly sale specials. Fortunately, when she left to go on to other things, I had the foresight to save them and used them again and again.

Nancy has a wonderful self-deprecating sense of humor. She created some lovely window displays. When I hear titles such as *The Girl with the Pearl Earring* or *The Piano Lessons*, which I still do at book clubs occasionally, I immediately think of her because she brought these and many other fine books to my attention.

Lisa was our most efficient employee, yet she was also a whiz at designing creative windows. Every employer should have an energetic staff member like her, one who anticipates what would be the most help and goes ahead and does it. A former editor, she also proofread my newsletters.

I felt so very fortunate to have had these dear people working for me at the store, as well as many other employees over the years.

Customers were always very appreciative of the Book Nook's staff. Time and time again, they commented, "You have the nicest help."

I did.

23. THE PRICE IS RIGHT: FAMILY HELP

During a recent family dinner at our house, I asked our younger daughter, Tricia, if she would bring me a serving spoon from the kitchen. "Sure, Mom," she said, adding in a sickeningly sweet tone, which she obviously thought was an exact imitation of my voice from over thirty years ago, "Tricia would love to help you pick out a book for your grandson; Tricia would be glad to wrap your books for you; Tricia would be happy to carry those books out to your car for you."

THE Book Nook's first workers were fourth graders: my daughter, Tricia, and her friend, Laura. They stamped the Book Nook's name on cashier pads and dusted shelves until they earned just enough money to buy ice cream cones, at which point they'd immediately quit their jobs until the next time they had a yearning for ice cream.

As my daughters grew older, even if they only dropped into the Book Nook to say hello — or to hit me up for money — they would spend an extra few minutes wrapping books for a customer or recommending children's books to a grandmother.

Both girls were lifesavers in the tedious job of stapling and folding the store's newsletters at home. It's not a coincidence that I stopped sending out newsletters about the time our younger daughter left for college.

Ginny, who was almost four years older than her sister, actually liked picking up and cleaning our house more than she liked working in the store. I realized her contribution was just as crucial — if not more so — than working at the store, and I began paying her for her help at home just as I did for any help in the store.

Tricia would work in the store when she needed some extra money, especially at Christmas time. She would also throw herself into designing delightful display windows. Her first attempt, when she was going to be a fifth grader, was a memorable beach summer reading theme. She propped her large rag doll, Annie, clad in a bikini and sunglasses, in a lounge chair under a big umbrella, surrounded by books. It was so outstanding, that for years, any time we had a particularly interesting window — usually created by a staff member — our regular customers automatically assumed, "Your daughter did your window again, I see."

Customers also remembered Tricia's special Peter Rabbit window in the spring of 1993. It won second place in a national bookstore window display contest, sponsored by Viking Penguin to highlight the 100th anniversary of the publication of *The Tale of Peter Rabbit.* Tricia actually grew a garden of onions and carrots in our window. Peter Rabbit's ears stuck out of a gardening can, and you could see Mr. McGregor's big leg coming from the side of a bookcase that resembled the inside of a toolshed, containing pots. A couple of boards leaned against it. Two customers, Laura and K.T. contributed garden tools for the window. We also posted in the window some of the children's entries for the Book Nook's *Tale of Mr. McGregor* contest. (*"What was I supposed to say, Go ahead, rabbit, eat my food. Let my family starve. I don't think so."*)

Often when my husband, Larry, or the girls as they grew older, stopped in to see me at the Book Nook, I'd ask them to watch the store for "just a couple of minutes" while I dashed to the bank, or to CVS for stationery supplies, or to Gershon's for take-out lunch or yes, I admit it, to Carole Bernardi's bakery to get a delicious brownie or a big cookie. They'd groan, but do it for me. Just ask any shop owner, if you run your store alone you're trapped there during business hours and will take advantage of friends, family, and even customers to escape.

Both my daughters hated answering the phone when I wasn't present since it probably would mean they'd be asked a question they couldn't answer. I'd suggest they take a number so I could call back immediately, but their solution was to pick up the phone the minute I was out of sight and call a friend; that way no calls could get through. Naturally, I wasn't thrilled with that method.

As each girl neared the end of her high school years, the store held less and less appeal. Dusting and shelving books were no longer fun. Each swore she'd do anything rather than work in the bookstore. It gave them a great incentive to find summer jobs, since I'd remark if they didn't find one, their default job would be at the Book Nook.

I was amused at Tricia's change of heart when during her Sophomore year at college, she landed a position at St. Lawrence University's bookstore, a plum job on campus. She had gotten it ahead of a number of other applicants since she had listed her experience working at the Book Nook.

Many of our steady customers grew to know Ginny and Tricia during their younger years, and even when the girls no longer lived at home, I still received many inquiries about them. On that horrendous 9/11 day, I was able to reassure several anxious callers that yes they were working in the city, but fortunately both worked in midtown, far from the Twin Towers. Our hearts broke for all those families who weren't so fortunate that day.

Of course, throughout the years, the biggest help to me was my husband, Larry. Many customers remarked that he looked like Phil Donohue (probably because of his premature white hair and his Irish good looks.) In 1983 he designed the layout of our first tiny store; then designed a new layout four years later when we moved into the larger store. He also handled more mundane matters, such as changing the ceiling fluorescent lights — no mean feat since some of the bulbs were eight feet in length.

He urged me from the first year to carry Adirondack Mountain Club books and other local interest books, a specialty that did very well. Each time Larry travelled North for business, he'd buy another small black bear figurine to bring back, which I placed among the Adirondack books. In 1988, he encouraged me to buy Bowker's Books in Print Plus computer program from our major wholesaler, Ingram, as well as their ordering program. It required an expensive updated computer that I felt we couldn't afford, but, of course, once installed, I realized that it was the best buying decision that we had ever made.

And, of course, Larry listened to me talk about the store and always had given his sensible, if sometimes painfully honest, opinion about my ideas, saving me from a few potentially disastrous mistakes. Also, everywhere he went, whether to his job as a Hobart Commercial Kitchen Equipment sales representative, or to church, or to a political meeting, he'd manage to squeeze in mention of the store, an invaluable salesman not only for his company but for the Book Nook.

24. Other American Booksellers' Conventions

(Part of an email to my mother)

I spotted in a sales catalog a New York State jigsaw puzzle. The minimum order was twenty-five puzzles. Normally too many of one item for me to buy for the store, but none of my wholesalers carried the puzzle so I couldn't try it out in a smaller quantity first. It seemed like such a sure winner, and, I decided to order it immediately after I returned from the ABA (The American Booksellers Association) Convention.

At the convention, I noticed the booth of the company that produced the different state puzzles and naturally checked out the New York State one. It included cities close to us: Albany, Troy, and Saratoga, but incredibly, the puzzle didn't show Schenectady.

Whew! Thank Heavens I hadn't ordered it yet. Not only would I have not sold any puzzles, but I would have had to listen to customers griping about our missing city. I can just hear them:

- *Don't they know that Schenectady is the city that used to "light the world" [General Electric Company] and used to "haul the world" [Alcoa Locomotive Company?]*

- *Don't they know that Thomas Edison, the inventor of the telephone and the founder of GE, lived here, as well as so many other famous scientists like Charles Steinmetz and Richard Feynman?*

- *Don't they know the first television broadcast was from Schenectady?*

I am so-o-o grateful not only not to have lost money on those puzzles but also to have escaped having to listen to the irate comments customers would have made about the omission of Schenectady on a New York State puzzle.

L ARRY and I attended many other American Booksellers' Conventions (ABAs) after my thrilling first one, usually managing to go every other year. I no longer was willing to spend time standing in lines for celebrities to autograph copies of their books although I still went to the celebrity breakfasts. Instead, I discovered gems from small presses; sifted through the children's picture books; checked out sidelines such as calendars; attended seminars, and above all; examined books that were scheduled to be printed in the fall. Selecting titles to order from the children's picture book display was particularly helpful.

I also discovered a press room. Here, the celebrity authors gave brief talks and answered reporters' questions. Feeling like an imposter with my last Book Chat column for a free throwaway paper, *The Niskayuna Journal*, tucked away in my handbag as my only credentials, my husband and I would join the audience of press representatives of *The New York Times*, *The Washington Post*, *The New Yorker*, *The Christian Science Monitor* and other equally lofty publications. In contrast to the breakfasts which several hundred people attended, only about thirty to forty media people were present so we really caught a close-up view of the celebrities. It was illuminating to see them and hear the questions posed to them in such a cozy session.

One time Stephen King followed Gloria Steinem. He told how his mother cleaned houses to support them when he was a boy. How she would bring home a box full of occult books from a secondhand bookstore and say, "I have here my mini vacation."

Another time Joseph Cotton, who was recovering from a stroke, tottered to the podium. He stammered, and his voice was too low to understand. However, as he continued to talk, the well-known dignified actor and showman began emerging as his voice grew stronger and his stature grew taller. Betty White came next. She was as vivacious in person as she was on the screen. Two minutes into her talk, she stopped suddenly and said, "Excuse me, I see my favorite of favorite actors sitting back there. I just *have* to see him." She rushed off the platform and raced to the back of the room to hug Joseph Cotton. Then she dashed back to finish her short talk and take questions.

At another session, Kaye Gibbons, the author of *Ellen Foster,* which I had hand-sold to many customers, kept referring to herself in her Southern accent as Bertha Kaye. I envisioned her publisher urging her to go with the more sophisticated name of Kaye Gibbons and wondered. If *Ellen Foster* had listed Bertha Kaye Gibbons as the author instead of Kaye Gibbons, would it have sold as many copies? I decided yes, the novel was so good, trivial matters like the author's name wouldn't have affected sales.

25. Every Bookstore Needs a Cat or Two

"Do you have Catwatching *by Desmond Morris?*

"No, I'm sorry, we're out, but I'd be glad to order it for you."

"No, thanks. Not enough time. My cat is giving it to my wife tomorrow for Mother's Day."

IN the 1990s, Oreo, a black cat with white markings splashed across his lower face, his neck and one leg, and Bright Eyes, a tiger cat with a circular white band around his neck and four white legs, took up part-time residence in the Book Nook. They didn't belong to us. They just visited two or more hours a day. Rosemary, a clerk at Henry's Dry-cleaning next door, claimed ownership. She provided them with food and water, took them to the vet for their shots and check-ups, and tried to make sure in freezing weather that they were inside for the night.

They often took naps among the books in one of the front windows or kept the mice away by prowling about in our back room. Since Rosemary fed them, I didn't give them any food, although I did put out water for them. If I had lots of customers or work that involved jumping up from my seat a lot, such as checking inventory, inevitably one of them would decide my lap was the perfect place to roost, purring contently or disgruntled when I had to dislodge him.

I didn't even provide a litter box. If they had to go out, they followed a customer who was leaving. If no one was going out, they merely sat looking up at the door, waiting for someone to enter or exit, or for me to notice them and let them out. In warm weather, I kept the front door open to make the store more inviting for people to stop in, and the cats came and left at will.

Oreo and Bright Eyes inspired me to do a cat book window one time, and often they stretched out in it, soaking up the sun's rays amid *the Garfield books, The Cat in the Hat, Millions of Cats, Catwatching,* and two mystery series: *The Cat Who* and the *Sneaky Pie Brown* books, much to the amusement of customers and passersby.

Other times, unerringly choosing people who were allergic to cats, they rubbed against their legs, ignoring their victims' efforts to escape. They avoided approaching cat-lovers, and if a customer came up to them and patted them, they tolerated it—barely.

When they first started coming around, I was startled one day when someone from the neighborhood recognized "Bibsey." A few days days later someone from Gershon's Deli recognized "Stripes" and looked around for "Blackie." Apparently they fed the cats scraps from the Deli. That very afternoon another person exclaimed, "Cat One and Cat Two, what are you doing here?" No wonder they looked so fat and contented.

One time Tony from Mailboxes, who had been picking up empty boxes from our store—he liked the sturdy book cartons—started backing his truck out of the parking space. He heard a noise from the back of his truck. He stopped to investigate, and the two cats jumped out, disappearing down the alleyway between the buildings. I assured him they were just casing the neighborhood and would be back shortly, probably after mooching for snacks.

They were a pleasant addition to the store with a minimum of fuss, except for those winter evenings when six o'clock came, the last customer had left, and I had finished the paperwork. Shifting to a Let's-get-home-as -soon-as-possible mode, I would gather up the bank deposit for the morning, my bag of books and catalogs, my handbag, and the key.

Henry's closed at 5:30, a half hour before my closing time, and about 5:20 Rosemary starting calling for the cats, but they often didn't show. Sometimes I'd exit my store to find Oreo and Bright Eyes outside looking up at me, shivering pitifully.

"Oh, all right." I'd grouse.

I'd have to turn around, go back into my store, and walk up the aisle to my desk, two cats trailing behind me. They'd sit, waiting patiently while I'd open the cash drawer, get out Henry's key, and make a quick call to Rosemary at home so she didn't have to return at eight or nine for another attempt to give the cats a warm shelter for the night. The cats proceeded me down the aisle and out the door and paused in front of Henry's while I locked the Book Nook and unlocked Henry's for them.

For all the times we executed this routine, those cats never once thanked me. They acted instead as if I should be grateful to serve them.

26. Bookaholics and Avoiders*

A mother was agonizing over a book to give her daughter's boyfriend for his birthday. He was visiting for the weekend. Just something to show that the parents had tuned in to his interests, she said. He liked the outdoors and sports. After several suggestions, she finally settled on 50 HIKES IN THE ADIRONDACKS by Barbara McMartin, convinced when I mentioned that my husband highly recommended McMartin's books.

One morning the following week, I was in the bank depositing the preceding day's proceeds and spotted my customer and asked her if the boyfriend had liked the book.

"Oh, he liked it all right," she said grimly. "We really gave him a book he loved."

"Isn't that what you wanted?"

"Yes, but our daughter's not talking to us because he liked the book so much he buried his face in it the whole time he was here and didn't pay any attention to her."

---

* From my article in *The American Bookseller Magazine*, June,1995 issue

As might be suspected, my favorite type of customer was the Bookaholic.

Bookaholics find it impossible to stop reading. They can't put a book down once they start. If they find a new author whom they like, they have to read everything that author has ever written. When they read a book review, they immediately wish they had that reviewed book in their hands to read; if the book review is about a book in the genre they particularly enjoy, they will rush to the library to borrow it, or to the bookstore to buy it.

Even if they stopped in "just to look," Bookaholics were always attracted to at least one book in the Book Nook, usually several, because of the author, the title, the subject matter, the picture on the cover, the jacket blurb, or even because it was finely bound, which meant to them that the words were probably treasures also. This, of course, is why bookstore owners encourage browsing.

Bookaholics can be subdivided into two categories: Bookaholics without money and Bookaholics with money; I loved them both equally--well, almost equally.

Bookaholics Without Money

Many Bookaholics on a tight budget tried to avoid temptation and rarely came into my store—although if they saw me elsewhere, they never failed to rave about how much they loved the store. They haunted the library instead.

Others made it an iron-clad rule just to buy paperbacks. However, if one of their favorite authors had come out with a new book, they might guiltily succumb and buy the hardcover. The usual year's wait until the paperback was issued seemed to stretch out to them as an eternity.

Bookaholics With Money

Bookaholics with money could afford to come in and indulge themselves by buying all the books they wanted. Once I tuned into the type of books they enjoyed, they'd take practically any book I showed them after the merest glimpse and more often than not they'd ask, "Do you have another one? It will make the perfect gift for my friend, too."

They'd often give me long hand-scrawled lists to order. If I suggested other books similar to the ones they requested, they'd usually responded without any hesitation, "Great. Add those to my order, too."

My only complaint about this type of customer — aside from the fact that I didn't have enough of them — was that they also had money to travel, so that they didn't stay home in Schenectady and buy books as often as they should.

Avoiders

The Avoider hadn't read a complete book from cover to cover since he was forced to thirty years ago in fourth grade. I usually could spot an Avoider as soon as he gingerly crossed the threshold. Instead of looking about as most customers did with an expectant air of finding delightful discoveries, he'd take a fearful, quick look at the bookcases, and then didn't glance at them for the rest of his visit, just as if he expected his grade school teacher to bellow out from behind one at any moment, "What's the plot of *Tom Sawyer*?"

When he finally spotted my desk near the middle of the store, he would determinedly make his way toward it. Meeting him halfway down the aisle, I'd ask him, "May I help you?" in as cheerful a voice as possible, knowing he had cast me in the role of Mrs. Read-This-Book-Or-Else–You-Are-Too-Stupid-For-Me-To-Waste-Any-More-Time-On-You, or, in other words, the ogre who turned him off reading so many years ago.

He'd muster up enough courage to ask for the technical book he needed about building a deck, or the book a friend asked him to pick up, or a book the teacher recommended he read to his son.

While finding the book for him or arranging to order it, I smiled a lot and made an inane comment about the weather so he knew I'm just as human — and bland — as the rest of God's creatures.

He'd relax only slightly and "Ma'am" me, and admit, "I don't get much time to read" to cover himself in case he was grilled on his literary knowledge. I'd try to give him a reassuring message, "Many people are too busy these days to read much." Sometimes I'd even go as far to admit. "They probably get a lot more accomplished than those of us who have our nose stuck in a book all the time."

With the Avoider I was not concerned with the sale. The main object was to try to make the bookstore and myself non-threatening enough, so that when he needed a book again, he'd come back without waiting another thirty years.

Perhaps, on a return visit, he'd overhear another customer buying a stack of westerns and raving to me how once he started a Louis L'Amour book, he couldn't put it down; and the former Avoider might just decide he'd like to try one himself -- just for the fun of it.

It has happened.

27. NICE MURDERERS*

"May I help you find something or did you just want to look around?" I asked a newcomer after she'd spent a few minutes browsing in the mystery section.

"Just looking. I can't stay long since I'm allergic to books."

"I'm sorry to hear that."

"Yes, bookstores make me ghastly ill."

"Oh?" I hadn't noticed before but she did look very pale and agitated.

"The oil in the chemicals in the binding affects me. It's like the Gulf War Syndrome. I start vomiting and gasping for breath. Sometimes I pass out."

"Er-uhm, this doesn't seem the place for you to be then."

"Oh, I can feel it coming on – most of the time anyway."

And the other times? It was the first time I was glad when a customer left without buying anything.

---

* Adapted from one of my *Niskayuna Journal* Book Chat columns.

M Y mother announced once that she only liked to read about "nice murderers" and although I never allowed her to forget such a ridiculous comment, I'll have to admit they're my favorite kind as well.

We don't want specific details where we'd be forced to visualize blood running, stomachs pumped out from poisoning attempts, or have to recognize that the victim was first raped. And we don't want drug addicts and the underworld cluttering up our murders.

No, we enjoyed a nice comfortable murder where the victim deserved it, entertaining suspects, and quaint detectives whom we like with maybe a little humor thrown in. First choice of setting: England. Second choice: New England.

Naturally the murderer had to be found and brought to justice — although if he or she were really considerate, he or she would fall off a cliff so we wouldn't have to envision a messy trial.

The old masters of this type of detective story, often referred to as "cozies," such as Dorothy Sayers, Margery Allingham, Ngaio Marsh, Rex Stout, Phoebe Atwood Taylor, Josephine Tey, and the grand dame of them all, Agatha Christie, set some pretty high standards, but there were many more recent writers during the years of the Book Nook who also wrote entertaining mysteries without wallowing in realism.

Many of my customers were mystery addicts. In fact if they read or spotted the latest book from an author whom they hadn't read before and if it looked interesting and/or I recommended it, they wanted to order all the earlier books by that author as well. Unfortunately the trend of big conglomerates taking over old name publishers continued, especially in the 1990s. Conglomerates were no longer as interested as the older, established publishers had been in the books as developers of ideas—as well as the bottom line, of course. They saw books as merely products. The numbers were the only thing that mattered to them. Blockbusters became essential and literary authors often fell by the wayside. The most idiotic practice, in my view, was to bring out a new hardcover by a mystery author with lots of fanfare, but to let the authors' preceding books lapse out of print, even if the new book was part of a series!

Many customers liked P.D. James' books. I read *An Unsuitable Job for a Woman* and liked it, but never seemed to get around to reading another of her books. Martha Grimes was another popular author whom my customers really liked and an author I always intended to read but to date haven't. The t-shirt saying spells out the problem: *So many books, too little time.*

The popular English author, P.D. James was featured at one of the American Bookseller Association's breakfasts, and I very much enjoyed her talk. With an atrocious English accent imitation, I repeated her words to customers. She talked about how authors often had amateur detectives helping out Scotland Yard. "However," she said, "If one of you booksellers were to fall out of your chair with a stiletto in your back, I am sure the Washington D.C. Police would not say, 'Thank heavens, we have the mystery writer, Mrs. James, present, who can help us solve the crime'." Her cultured English accent made her words seem particularly funny.

I shared other tidbits of information about mystery authors with customers.

For example, Anne Perry, the author of the excellent Victorian mysteries with a feminist slant, had committed murder herself at the age of fifteen in New Zealand. She and another girl killed the friend's mother because the mother wanted to move back to England, thereby separating the two best friends. Perry was released after five years with the provision she never see the other girl again. You would have thought she would have avoided any association with murders, even the fictitious kind.

There was a national hunt in 1926 for Agatha Christie, who had disappeared under mysterious circumstances. Her car was found at the top of a quarry, and she was feared dead. She eventually was discovered at a resort hotel using the name of her husband's lover. The poor woman had been in a depressed state because of her mother's death, then her husband had asked her for a divorce.

In honor of Agatha Christie's 100th birthday, which her American publisher was celebrating in 1990, we held a mystery writing contest. Instructions were to write the first page of a mystery. A local radio station read the three winning entries. As I recall we only had about thirty entries, not the overwhelming response we had with our last two children's contests. Still, it resulted in some free publicity. I made a mistake in not having a professional writer as a judge as we did for *The Tale of Mr. McGregor* contest. Afterwards, I realized we had completely missed an outstanding entry. I still feel guilty about it.

I often posted in the store a list of mysteries along different themes: academics, bookstores, cats, dogs, horses, cooking, crafts, and detectives in foreign countries.

Our most requested mysteries were Elizabeth George books about Inspector Lynley, set in England. Amazingly, the author is an American. One of the most popular lighter mystery authors was M.C. Beaton who wrote about Hamish Beamish, an unambitious, lazy Scots policeman, and Agatha Raisin, a dynamic, aggressive public relations agent. In 1998, Alexander McCall Smith wrote about an unusual detective, "traditionally built" Mma Ramostswe, who opened her No.1 Ladies Detective Agency in Botswana. She admired Agatha Christie. New books in the series—twenty-five at last count!—are still being produced today.

28. GUESSING TITLES: DENSE OR PSYCHIC?

"Book Nook, Judy Hoff speaking."

"You said 'Judy', right?"

"That's right. May I help you?"

"Yes, I'm J.A's mother. I'm doing a crossword puzzle, and she said you'd know. Gordimer?"

"Nadine?'

"What?"

"Nadine, N-a-d-i-n-e, is the only Gordimer, I know. She writes about South Afr – "

"Nadine! That fits. Thanks. She said you'd know."

Click.

VERY often customers supplied us with the sketchiest information when they inquired about a book.

"Let me have that boat book by Ken Foley."

"Ken Foley?" Never having heard of this author, I began typing his name on the computer.

"You know. It's a spy book."

"Ah-h-h. You mean, Ken *Follett*."

"Does he write spy books, too?"

The trick is to forge doggedly ahead. "I wasn't aware Ken Follett had a new book out about boats, but let me check out his titles—"

"Come on! You must know the book. Everybody's talking about it. President Reagan loved it."

"You don't mean the one about the lost Russian submarine, *The Hunt for the Red October* by Tom Clancy?"

"Yes, of course."

Another frustrating conversation was with a woman looking for such an unusual sideline that I couldn't figure out why she expected to find it in a bookstore. I thought she was going to attack me, she was so aggravated by my denseness.

"Do you have any gynecology sheets?"

"Excuse me?"

"You know, those gynecological sheets?"

"I can order books for you on gynecology."

"No, no, I need the sheets."

Now people have asked us for some pretty strange things unrelated to books, but I had to be missing something. Why was she was coming to a bookstore for those white paper things medical personnel spread over women's bottom halves before a GYN exam?

"I'm sorry, I'm still not following you. Could you describe them to me."

"You must know, those tables where you put down your family tree."

"Oh! You mean "genealogy."

"That's what I said. "Gynecological sheets." I could tell it was a real effort for her to restrain from adding, "You idiot!"

Unfortunately, I didn't have genealogy sheets either.

Other times, a person who ordinarily didn't read that much for pleasure happened upon a book once that captured his interest so much that he actually plowed through the entire thing. Not realizing the sheer volumes of great books in the universe that mainly go unread, he couldn't comprehend that I, who owned a bookstore, and therefore should know everything about all books, had not heard of this wonderful book. What was even more incomprehensible to him, since I couldn't find it in books in print, I indicated it might be out of print.

He was convinced if he just kept feeding me details, I'd remember this outstanding book. "It's about men in blue and purple striped pajamas with carrots for heads in outer space, and they discover another planet with only women. They wear red and pink pajamas and have tomatoes for heads.

"Sounds fascinating, but I haven't read it. I actually don't read much science fict — "

"But this is a superior book. You *must* have read it. Let me tell you some more details…"

"I'm certain I would remember reading about men in purple and blue pajamas with tomatoes for their heads."

"That's carrots for the men. Tomatoes for the women. Are you sure you don't remember reading it? Once they land on this new planet they do some spectacular things, and the women are no slouches in fighting them off either. Let me tell you some more…'

Like a ten-year-old determined to tell you every detail of a movie he has just seen, this customer would be off and running, while I prayed for any interruption — the meter man would do nicely.

Then, on the other hand, there were customers, who were convinced I was psychic because with the merest mention of a code word in a title, I could blurt out the title and author often before they were finished speaking.

Clues such as the following made it easy to place the book in their hands:

1. The strong man book?
2. Oprah's cookbook?
3. The tell-all restaurant book?
4. The mall book about raising teenagers?

5. The woman and the wolf book?

6. The bridge book?

7. The vegetarian cookbook from an upstate NY restaurant?

8. Expecting a baby book?

9. The intelligent woman book?

10. The local priest book?

There was nothing psychic or even remarkable about it, of course. These books were bestsellers and the same titles were inquired about over and over.

Now you know my secret.

In case you didn't recognize all of the names by the clues given, here are the books.

1. *Iron John* by Robert Bly.

2. *In the Kitchen with Rosie* – not by Oprah, but by her cook, Rosie Daley.

3. *Kitchen Confidential* by Anthony Bourdain.

4. *Get Out of my Life, But First Take Me and Cheryl to the Mall* by Anthony E. Wolf.

5. *Women Who Run with the Wolves* by Clarissa Pinkola Estes.

6. *The Bridges of Madison County* by Robert James Waller.

7. *The Moosewood Cookbook* by Mollie Katzen.

8. *What to Expect When You are Expecting* by Heidi Murkoff.

9. *Smart Women, Foolish Choices* by Connell Cowan and Melvyn Kinder.

10. *Joshua* by Joseph Girzone.

Incidentally, *Joshua*, a novel about Jesus returning to earth as a carpenter in an upstate New York town, turned out to be a publishing phenomenon. It was a self-published book (1983) at a time when most self-published books usually did not sell more than a few copies to family and friends. The first time its author, Joseph Girzone, a retired priest, appeared at the Book Nook to autograph his book, we had the biggest crowd for any author, before or after. Father Joseph Girzone managed to sell fifty thousand copies on his own before the book was picked up in 1987 by Macmillan Publishers! According to Wikipedia, *Joshua* and its sequels eventually sold over a million copies.

29. You Want *Me* to Make a Speech?

I'd been asked to be one of the speakers at an American Association of University Women's program about multiculturalism. Children's literature was my topic. A middle-aged women came forward before we began and told me, "You're the only reason I came tonight."

She approached me again after the program and raved about my talk. Her enthusiasm was so catching that visions of my own book review television circuit, starting with Oprah, flitted across my mind.

Then she had to drop me back to reality.

"By the way, since you're a bookseller, I'd like to talk to you about my son, the author. If you bought several copies of his books, I know you'd sell ..."

ONE of the great joys of graduating from college was my belief that I would never, ever have to make another oral report.

After all, if, when you're faced with an audience, no matter how small, your voice sounded as shrill as that of an adolescent and your thought processes didn't boot up beyond the level of a one-year-old; would you want to make a speech?

I certainly didn't, that's for sure, until I opened the Book Nook. Then I volunteered, demonstrating the lengths I was willing to go to promote the store.

My first talks were agony, and even though they never went as poorly as feared, a tension headache before and during the speech usually developed into an upset stomach hours later.

As the years went by, speaking was no longer the painful ordeal it had been, and to my surprise there were even some talks I enjoyed giving. The experience did bring a bit of wisdom, which I'd like to share with anyone who dreads talking in public.

1. If asked to give a three-minute speech, give a three-minute speech — or better yet, a two and a half minute speech.

One of my first speeches was at a meeting of the Schenectady Business and Professional Women's Association (BPW) describing how I had started the Book Nook. The previous speaker, who also owned her own business, had talked on at length about how her husband, or "Daddy" as she called him, helped her so much by cleaning the house or having dinner ready when she came home. She went on and on about how wonderful "Daddy" was at home, but didn't describe much about her business. As I listened enviously, I wished I could find the words to convey that she virtually had a supportive "wife" at home, something men had for centuries, but something for which most working women even in the late 1980s still futilely yearned. I couldn't form the right words, but as I stood up, a cliched remark suddenly occurred to me. "I just have one question," I said, looking about the room. "Does Daddy have a brother?"

A very old line, but it received as much laughter as if it were original.

Unfortunately, my talk went downhill from there. The moderator had announced that since we were running late, the numerous speakers would be limited to three minutes each. She actually had an egg timer. Not having had much experience, I thought maybe I could squeeze my six minute speech into a three minute one by just talking twice as fast. In the last part, I had included a few words of thanks to the members for the support they had shown my store. I felt it was vital to mention since I was genuinely grateful. However, I was concentrating so hard on the message that when the sand ran out, the moderator had to come over and tap me on the shoulder to get my attention. I still babbled on, "I just want to say, thank —"

It finally sunk in as she kept tapping with increasing force that she meant, Stop talking NOW! I broke off abruptly and slunk back to my seat.

Afterwards, consolation for a sore shoulder and the humiliating ending came, as a couple of people were interested enough in my talk to call me later asking advice about starting their own businesses.

2. Take several deep breaths before your presentation.

My preparation beforehand of taking deep breaths kept me from actually hyperventilating as a guest on a radio show. My voice did get shrill, but at least, I wasn't gasping for air. When he had asked me to be on his show, the moderator had gone over the two topics he wanted me to discuss: (1) the benefits of reading aloud to children and (2) children's authors who lived in the community. I was figuring a twenty-minute discussion at least.

The interview was conducted over the phone instead of at the studio, which made me even more nervous than usual.

As soon as we were on the air, the host introduced me and covered himself the importance of reading aloud for several minutes, giving me no chance to offer my thoughts on the topic. Then he asked me about local authors. I didn't have more than a couple of sentences out of my mouth about C.S. Adler and was all set to mention some of her books when he interrupted to say we'd have to move on to other authors.

It was about a three-minute spot, if that. I did manage to talk (barely), but my timing was completely off, and I've never had the courage to listen to a tape of the show.

I should have been prepared with a shorter version, perhaps just mentioning the large number of talented authors in the area, given their names, and then if there were time, expanding to some of the authors' works. From then on, I always asked the estimated length of my interview.

On a different radio station where the pace was more relaxed and the host asked me to provide her with some questions ahead of time, I performed much better. We talked for several minutes, and I even winged some questions from a couple of callers. Oh, all right, so one of them was a carefully coached friend who asked the question I'd written out for her. One should be prepared after all!

3. Don't hand out any items that might be more fascinating than your talk.

In one of my first talks to a book club, I handed out books ahead of time to the members, whom I assumed would look them over and pass them along as I talked about each title. The problem was everyone kept leafing through the books, nudging their neighbor to look at the

pictures, and even reading parts of the jacket blurbs to each other. Any moment, I expected an audience member to order me, "Quiet! We want to read these books." After that, I just handed out lists, noting only titles, authors, and prices so people could check off books that they might like to buy as I talked about them.
4. Don't avoid popular topics.

Don't avoid talking about something just because it's well known. I had several months to prepare for my talks about Jane Austen, scheduled for two consecutive Schenectady Library sessions, about forty minutes each with a question and answer period afterwards. Despite the enjoyment of absorbing tons of information about the author's life and books, as the time came closer I still felt ill prepared to give an adequate speech, having never talked that long, or to so many people in a live audience, as well as knowing it was going to be taped for the Schenectady public TV station.

I was growing increasingly panicked as the time grew closer, but luckily I approached a friendly book group whom I had discussed new novels with a year before, and they agreed to help me. There was so much material to cover that even though I concentrated on just one book and different aspects of Jane Austen's life for each session, I rushed through the material with them. Fortunately, the kind members made me feel the material was fascinating and helped me to slow down and look at the audience. One member of the group, Ann Tetrault, gave me the most helpful suggestions about public speaking techniques. With this help and some tips from books on public speaking, I was able to get through the library talks. They certainly weren't the best talks given at the library, but they weren't the worst either.

The biggest mistake I made was not talking about most people's favorite Austen book, *Pride and Prejudice*. I figured people were probably too familiar with it, and talked the first week about the less popular *Emma* and the second week about *Persuasion*. I had plenty to say about each book and also about Jane Austen's life, but everyone was disappointed that I didn't talk about *Pride and Prejudice*. The sessions would have been much better if the books discussed had been *Pride and Prejudice* and *Persuasion*. People do enjoy discussions about books they love.

5. Try to go with the flow.

Somehow, I ended up with my very own taped show on the local Schenectady public television station. I did a series of half hour shows with local authors and one with Book Nook customers talking about "cozy mystery" books. Even though it was taped, it didn't mean that if there were goofs it could all be re-taped. No, I had to go through the whole thirty minutes without stopping. On the very first show I misinterpreted the director's signal that we were through and began winding up, only to realize from his frantic motions that we had ten more minutes to get through. TEN MORE LONG MINUTES! I said "Oops, sorry about that, we're not done after all." and desperately came up with another question. And another. And another. But there was no going back and re-taping. This was a low budget station to beat all low budget television. Usually, I had two guests, one for each fifteen minute segment. The director had the guest who wasn't on the air, manning the camera for the other segment! He ignored my comments that it was completely unacceptable, that guests shouldn't be manning the camera. My husband still remembers with amusement that one of the authors, Sister Dorothy, a nun who had written an inspirational spiritual book, good-naturedly took over the camera after her segment. Some of my other guests weren't as happy about it.

6. If you talk about a subject you love and the audience loves it as well, you can't go too far wrong.

After all the talks I'd given about books—new books, local author books, children's books, mystery books, multi-cultural books, gift books for the holidays, books about independent women to name a few—it took an invitation from the Scotia Reading Circle to provide me with the perfect topic. "Talk about your favorite books."

So simple. So much fun. No need to outline my talk. No need to have notes other than just a list of titles, which included: *Fried Green Tomatoes at the Whistle Stop Cafe, West with the Night, Ellen Foster, A Year in Provence, At Home in Mitford, The Widow's Mite* (short stories with a warning to avoid the last one, a very dark story in contrast to the others), *The Ladies No. 1 Detective Agency, and Snow Falling on Cedars.*

Since the club members were such book-lovers, they overlooked the tangents and the groping for the right word. Of course, their positive reaction to me may also have been a little influenced by the $5 Book Nook gift certificate I gave to each member just before my talk. Hey! Experience is the best teacher. I was learning how to give better and better talks and to please my audience more and more. If I had to include bribery among my methods, so be it.

That brings me to my last piece of advice about giving a successful talk.

7. Bribery helps to insure a receptive audience.

30. Booksellers Go Berserk at My Last National Book Convention

(Overheard at the 1995 Book Convention)

Author to Agent: Wow! I had always thought booksellers were a mild-mannered lot, but this crew is out for blood.

I<small>N</small> 1995, although we didn't know it at the time, Larry and I attended our last national book convention in Chicago. It actually was no longer the ABA (the American Booksellers Association) Convention, but was now the BEA (Book Expo of America) Convention. The ABA had turned over its convention to Book Expo to run. Unfortunately, although Book Expo were experts in running conventions, they knew zilch about independent booksellers. The busy convention floor looked the same as usual. It was crammed with booths from publishers and presses selling books that were coming out the next fall, as well as many sideline businesses. The only difference from the normal ABA were the huge—and I do mean huge—numerous red banners extending across the entire ceiling, displaying the words:

AMAZON.COM AMAZON.COM AMAZON.COM

Normally mild-mannered booksellers turned livid. We couldn't have been more furious if we were NRA members with signs overhead at their convention saying, "BAN ALL GUNS."

To booksellers, it was bad enough to know that our customers could order all *The New York Times* Bestsellers at Amazon at 30% off, but it infuriated us to see these banners in Chicago where we had planned as usual to have a fun, working holiday. Before, we knew that the ABA always had the independent booksellers' best interests at heart. The ABA had been battling superstores and Amazon for us, and while it might have seemed like a losing battle, they actually had won some victories. Most recently they had won a lawsuit against Viking Penguin for its favoritism to superstores. All member independent bookstores who had sold any of their books during the preceding year, would at a minimum receive $1000 in compensation. What's more the check came through with amazing speed. So to have the red Amazon signs flapping over our heads at this apparent safe haven made our blood boil.

Ordinarily, I had too much else to see, to bother to attend the ABA annual meeting, but I heard so many curses, threats, and rumblings, it was obvious that this year's meeting was going to be full of fireworks, and I didn't want to miss the show. As I entered the large meeting room and took a seat near the back, so I could escape if it became too ugly, I saw on all sides booksellers ready to confront the organizers. They had thick notes of what they planned to shout, crammed in hands that were already thrusting about as if fighting a duel.

Promptly on time, the President of the ABA called the meeting to order, and after remarkably few words of greeting, introduced the spokeswoman for the Book Expo group, giving her the floor. I felt so sorry for this hapless woman as she started to open her mouth. She probably didn't have anything to do with the banners, yet they were throwing her into the lions' den, but I soon realized she was equal to the task. Her first words were something along the lines of: "We are so so sorry. We should never have taken Amazon's ads. A TREMENDOUS MISTAKE on our part. And something like this will NEVER, EVER happen again. We will be sure in the future to run everything by a committee of booksellers chosen by the ABA." She went on along these lines for several more minutes repeating the basic apology of how the BEA realized how much they had goofed, that they were extremely sorry, and the steps they were going to take to avoid such a horrendous gaffe from recurring.

I could feel the tension from the audience slowly deflating. When the BEA woman asked for questions, several members got up to speak briefly, one after the other basically saying the same thing. They had come prepared for a battle, but conceded now there was nothing to fight.

They sounded disappointed.

31. THE CHRISTMAS ANGEL

Having just finished wrapping both a children's board book and a 365 page-a-day Dilbert business calendar, I turned the packages over, ready to mark on the bottom the recipients' names for my customers.

She stopped me. "Don't bother, I'll be able to tell them apart."

"Are you sure?" I asked. "They're quite similar in size."

She was sure.

She came in a few days later. "I should have listened to you,"

Apparently, when my customer's boss unwrapped the board book, GUESS HOW MUCH I LOVE YOU, it turned out to be the highlight of the Holiday Office Party.

FIVE minutes of two in the afternoon four days before Christmas, I was cashing out the line of people at the register as quickly as possible, so I could get to the customers who needed assistance finding presents. Sue was helping me, but she had to leave at two, and I was worried about how I was going to handle everyone on my own. That's when a woman, whom I didn't know, came up to me. "Excuse me, I smell gas."

"Gas?" I said.

"Yes. There is definitely a smell of gas."

"I don't smell gas. Does anyone else smell gas?"

No one did.

"There is a definite smell of gas."

"Please, we are so busy here."

"I do smell gas, and I am never wrong about these things."

"That will be $43.49," I told my customer, grateful she didn't want her books wrapped.

"I am not leaving until you take care of this," the same woman persisted again.

Sue said she'd stay, while I rushed downstairs to check the furnaces. The basement contained an old gas boiler for two units in the building and a gas furnace for one unit, which I had replaced three years before. I sniffed the area around both of them. Nothing.

I hurried back upstairs. "I didn't smell anything downstairs." *There, I checked it out so that should satisfy you. Just go now!*

"There is a definite gas smell over here. Come here and smell."

Reluctantly, I went to the wall where she was standing. Damn it! I did catch a faint whiff of gas.

I called Niagara Mohawk. "Okay, they are on their way." I looked around to see if the woman was finally satisfied, but she had disappeared—along with quite a few potential customers.

Within ten minutes, the Niagara Mohawk woman showed up. I pointed to the basement stairs and turned back to the one remaining customer.

Within a very short time, the Niagara Mohawk worker was upstairs again, frowning. "Ma'am, please come downstairs with me." *Not good.* I grabbed the cash register key, locked the front door, and dashed downstairs after her. Fortunately, there seemed to be a lull in customers entering the store. The mention of a gas smell before had scared off those in the store. The phone was ringing, but the machine could handle that.

She had taken the bottom plate off the boiler and showed me that the burner pan with the row of flames had dropped to the bottom of the furnace. *Yikes! Definitely not good.*

"Very dangerous. Ma'am, I'm turning off the furnace, turning off the gas, and locking the box. You'll have to call us to unlock the box and get the gas back on."

"How long does that take to get someone to come back and unlock it?"

"I am not sure. Sometimes awhile. A few days."

"A few days! Christmas is in four days. these are my busiest days of the year. I can't be without heat!" Even

though it wasn't one of the coldest spells we seemed to go through every winter when the temperature sunk below zero for three or more days in a row, it still dipped below freezing every night.

"I'm sorry. Safety comes first."

She went out to her truck to get some tools. I called Adams Heating Co., who had put in the new hot air furnace for me and explained the situation about the boiler. "You definitely don't want them to put a lock on the gas. Could take days to get them back to unlock it." Adams said they would be there before eight the next morning to put in a new boiler. The Niagara Mohawk woman had come back inside and heard me confirming the time. Fortunately she said she wouldn't lock the box after all since Adams was coming right away to put in a new furnace. Without the lock, Adams could turn the gas back on themselves. *Whew. The only thing that had gone right that afternoon.*

As promised, the new boiler was installed the next morning. That day and forever more, I have given thanks for our annoying, persistent, anonymous customer. It would not only have been our store that would have been devastated by an explosion and/or fire but also our tenants: Henry's Dry Cleaning Store and the family in the apartment upstairs. One of Henry's clerks often brought her little girl with her to work, and the tenant living upstairs had three children!

I still shudder to think how close we all had come to disaster.

People when they hear the story often ask me details about the women who refused to leave until I had called Niagara Mohawk, but I am sorry to say, I have no memory of her. Old? Young? I didn't notice. Color of hair? A blank. Stylish or drab clothing? Nothing. Height? Medium maybe—or maybe not.

Yet, I will never forget her.

32. Money Isn't Everything[*]

A customer and I were discussing the new Barnes and Noble that had moved into the shopping center, Mohawk Commons, just five minutes' drive from the Book Nook. "They have so many books," I griped.

"Yes, they may have more books," he agreed and hastened to reassure me, "but they don't have better books."

INDEPENDENT bookselling is a very positive occupation, which probably explains why there were so many of us in such a low profit field.

Of course, there were the obvious benefits for any booklover: conversations with other readers, meeting authors, and an unending supply of reading—kept at home, of course, since, contrary to popular belief, booksellers don't have time to read on the job.

---

[*] Adapted from one of my Book Chat columns in the *Niskayuna Journal*

Other less conspicuous benefits also made working in a bookstore enjoyable; mainly, the very special people we met in the store.

We saw:

- Youngsters whose parents had to bribe them in order to drag them away from the allure of books. *"Michael, come now. We have to go. There'll be no time for ice cream if you don't come. Now!"*

- Teachers who were driven to share their love of reading with students and often dug deeply into their own pockets for books to place in their classrooms. One teacher told me that she had gathered her year's receipts together for income tax purposes and was shocked to discover that she had spent over $1700 on children's books.

- A live wire sixty-five-year-old, who celebrated her birthday by buying $65 worth of books to donate to her church's children's library.

- Niskayuna High School students who raised several thousand dollars for three years in a row in December in order to put books in the hands of poor children.

- The Northeast Parent and Child Society, one of the organizations that benefited from a donation of book money from the high school program named above, sent young teens in to select their own books. Their teacher told me many of these youngsters had never been in a bookstore before. Typical of this age group, they seemed mostly drawn to horror books. Many of the girls had a hunger for poetry, particularly love poetry, and I'll always remember the boy who chose the thick Civil War book by Geoffrey Ward. He couldn't believe anyone would give him something that spectacular and began pouring over it even before leaving the store. One boy with a reading disability, after much thought and discussion with his teacher and me, chose a how to draw animals book. Several weeks later, he returned to give me a booklet with his carefully drawn illustrations of animals he had learned to do from the book.

We also saw:

- A reading group of delightful elderly ladies who often chose books by Sophocles or Plato for their selections. Some of the members were disappointed, feeling that their group was slowing down since they were not reading the material in the original Greek.

- A teenager, obviously a loner and probably on drugs, often came into the store and seemed drawn to occult books. However, eventually he instead began looking at books on architecture, leading me to have a glimmer of hope for his future.

- The eager participation of 780 youngsters from several different local schools in a writing and drawing contest the Book Nook held in honor of Arnold Lobel's work, where the prize was not for individuals, but books for their school classroom. They obviously had labored just as hard over their entries as if the prizes were going directly to them.

- A volunteer at the county jail who bought books with her own money to fill in gaps in the library there, such as books on pregnancy or certain fiction authors.

- A minister who came in clutching a $50 gift certificate from his congregation. He looked as delighted as a child in a bike shop selecting his first two wheeler.

- A grade school librarian, who started a very successful program at Glencliff School, based on the national program "1000 Books." The idea was that pre-schoolers by the time they began school should have been exposed through reading aloud to at least 1000 books. Busy parents were delighted to run in and pick up a bag of ten pre-selected paperback picture books at the school library. They were sure to find that more than half of them would appeal to their preschoolers.

On bad days competition seemed to be bearing down on us from all sides: discounters, chains, book clubs, superstores, warehouses, and mail order. It seemed that books were sold everywhere: over television, on the internet, in supermarkets, schools, drugstores, churches, synagogues, directly from the publisher, and in every gift shop. I sometimes felt as if the prediction that independent bookstores would soon become obsolete was inevitable.

I had recently discovered, from going over some family papers, that my mother's grandfather invented and patented a nifty new type of whale oil lamp in the nineteenth century. Unfortunately, his timing was off. Gas lamps were replacing whale oil lamps. On rare gloomy days, I felt an affinity with him.

However, that was only on rare bad days. On most days working in such an uplifting environment, I felt particularly fortunate, especially when someone would open the front door and call in. "Thank you. That book you recommended for my stuffy aunt, *The Shell Seekers*; she just loved it!"

How many people work doing what they love every day? And in how many other businesses do customers make a special trip back to report how grateful they are that you recommended they buy your product?

33. REFLECTIONS WHILE SLOWING DOWN

(E-mail one very slow, snowy morning to my mother)

So, the store's not making any money. Yet, where else would I have a discussion with an eighty-plus-year-old smooth-talking lawyer, who, when he's in an ordering mode, will call me several times a day? In other words, every time he gets a new thought.

Today, for example, I've already heard from him five times — all before 11:00 a.m.

Call #1: Jud-ith, that book, THE ELEMENTS OF STYLE by Strunk and White, is excellent. Why didn't you tell me?

Me: I did when you were first asking about grammar books a couple of weeks ago, but you said you knew it and sounded very sure you didn't want it — it was for writers' only. (I had, of course, made several attempts to assure him that it was for everybody interested in grammar, not just professional writers, but he wasn't listening.)

Call #2: Jud-ith, I want to order two copies of that book.

Me: Okay, will do. They should be here tomorrow afternoon. I think it's a great book myself. I like to write, and I try to re-read it every few years. Still haven't absorbed it completely even though it's a slim volume.

<u>*Call #3*</u>*: Jud-ith why didn't you tell me you are a writer? I'd have listened to you.*

Me: Well, I've had very little published.

Him: But you're a writer. Means you know grammar. (I didn't tell him that liking to write didn't automatically make me a grammar expert.)

<u>*Call #4*</u>*: Jud-ith, you should know that my first reaction is to say "no" to everything. You gotta keep pitching me.*

Me: I'm a lousy salesperson. People say "No" to me, I take them at their word.

Him: No. No. No. You're a good salesperson. That's called soft sell – that's <u>supposed</u> to be very good. (His tone indicated he really couldn't believe that, but he is a natural schmoozer.)

<u>*Call #5*</u>*: Jud-ith, I've only read a few pages of the book so far. What do you think the rule is regarding ending a sentence with a preposition? An expert grammarian friend of mine says it's very wrong.*

Me: I believe it's acceptable informally, but in formal writing or speech, it's generally not approved of.

Him: You just did it! You ended a sentence with a preposition.

Me (dryly): Ri-ght-t-t.

Him: Oh! I get it. Ha. Ha. (Pause) Last night a city councilman made a speech and ended two sentences with a preposition. I didn't think it was right.

I told him what he wanted to hear, namely, that technically the councilman wasn't correct, but after he hung up, I realized I should have said, "If ending a sentence with a preposition is the worst error a politician makes, we all can consider ourselves lucky." The morning's not over yet, and I'm sure I'll have a chance to work it in with Call Number Six.

UNSURPRISINGLY, when I saw the movie, *You've Got Mail*, in 1999, the plot really resonated with me. The Meg Ryan character, owner of a beloved, small, independent children's bookstore, was being forced out of business by Tom Hank's mega bookstore moving into her neighborhood. This mirrored my own problems.

The Book Nook had been able to survive up until then, even with both a Barnes and Noble and a Borders in Colonie, which were less than a half hour's drive away. It had also survived the competition several years before from another bookstore, an independent children's specialty one, that had set up operations just three blocks away. That store lasted for two and a half years. However, the arrival of a Barnes and Noble in the latter part of the 1990s in the Mohawk Commons just five minutes away, was another matter. It really cut into our December Holiday business which provided 35% of our yearly income. Orders, too, more and more often were handed to me on Amazon printouts with a 30% discount for bestsellers. Such gestures made me feel like a charity case, even while I deeply appreciated the loyalty. Meanwhile, our tenant, a drop-off branch of Henry's Dry Cleaning Store, which helped pay the building's high property taxes, pulled out, and there was no other tenant ready to replace Henry's. Schenectady's major employer, General Electric Company, had been relocating thousands of jobs from Schenectady, drastically affecting the local economy.

To get back to the movie, most people—or women at least—didn't get it. They told me, yes, it was sad Meg had to give up her bookstore, but gaining Tom Hanks made it worth it. Much as I like Tom Hanks, I didn't feel he was sufficient compensation for Meg losing her bookstore! I had been married to the love of my life for over three decades by then, and was slowly coming to the realization that I was going to have to give up the other love of my life, the Book Nook.

My family got it, of course. In fact, our younger daughter, Tricia, then working in New York City, went to see *You've Got Mail* with a bunch of her friends. She ended up sobbing uncontrollably in the middle of the movie, disturbing her friends and other patrons who were there to enjoy a fun, romantic film.

Fortunately, the store was not as badly off as some bookstores I had heard about with thousands of dollars in unpaid inventory costs. That is, *if*, we could sell the building. Our asking price was less than we had paid for it for because property values in Schenectady were dropping at the time. We placed a huge sign across part of the Book Nook's facade:

BUILDING FOR SALE

Yet, there was little action. Customers came in perturbed that a nasty landlord was going to put us out on the street. We had no nibbles, other than from a couple of dreamers who didn't actually have money to buy the building.

We were in limbo most of the time, trying to carry on as usual. I was extremely careful about new books I ordered for the store, only selecting those that should be snatched up instantly. I told people that when the store closed, gift certificates would be worthless, but customers often wanted to buy them anyway. I put a three-month expiration date at the bottom of the certificate so the recipients would be warned.

Despite the sign, I don't think many of our customers realized, or at least faced the fact, that we were going to close. Even I forgot about it for days at a time.

As the months and then years crept by with no offers to buy the building containing the Book Nook, there was a lot of time for reflection. Although I felt I had plunged into opening the store with too little capital and no retailing experience, I began to understand that my background had helped me enormously in being able to keep the store open for almost two decades. Most importantly, of course, was my love of books which had been encouraged in my youth by my mother's own love of books, and by my father, who had built a platform high up in a backyard maple tree so that I could combine my two favorite activities: reading and tree-climbing. I am not sure whether other high school English courses at the time gave excerpts from English literature throughout the ages and emphasized knowing titles and authors, the way mine did, but when a customer would come in and mention Isaac Walton (which surprisingly happened every year or so), I could say without any hesitation, "the author of *The Compleat Angler*?" without having ever read a page of the book. In college, I probably should have been an English major but was only an English minor, which meant my literature courses were electives and for fun. Aside from a Shakespeare course, I chose courses about novels, and usually had read the entire semester's worth in the first two weeks. Study of these books meant I was able to hold my own in any rare discussions in the store of *classics such as Crime and*

Punishment or the symbolism in *The Great Gatsby* with the most learned of my customers.

Painfully shy, and an only child until my brother came along when I was seventeen, I spent a lot of time observing adults, starting with my mother from a cultured middle-class background and my father, a blue collar worker. I found it interesting that my father, who had spent most of his school years playing hooky so he could ride his horse, usually grasped new concepts much faster than my Mount Holyoke-educated mother.

These observations of my parents and other adults helped me understand different types of people as did various positions I held, such as my interviewing job and then supervisory job with New York State. At a part time real estate job, I'd absorbed the importance of positive marketing. And the typing skill acquired at my last job meant once I figured out what I wanted to say in my Book Chat column or in composing a press release, my fingers flew across the computer. Even the memory of the two worst jobs, the typing one and an equally boring dead end job at an insurance company, helped me. When I was vacuuming the store or doing paperwork, I recognized that these tedious tasks played a small part to enable me to spend the rest of my time doing what I loved most: meeting fellow book-lovers, surrounded by books.

I poached the idea of placing a rolling cart near the sales counter from the memory of a similar one at a part-time library job I'd held several years before. Customers could dump books on it they no longer were considering, and I could also place there newly unpacked books before shelving them. This small space turned out to be the Book Nook's most valuable real estate. That was the first-place customers usually checked when they came into the store, often finding treasures among the hodgepodge of books piled there. It had the added advantage of cutting down on the number of books needing to be shelved.

I also had plenty of time to think about what I should have done differently, such as listening to customers who liked the idea of a rewards program. They liked the thought of getting a free book after buying ten to twelve books at the store. In the days before the existence of a computerized program that now takes care of figuring out average costs, it just sounded too time-consuming. A free book after buying ten books, also meant that the total of all eleven books would come to about 9% off each book. I felt rotating different sections of the store each month at 20 to 25% off were actually better bargains. However, as I stated in my opening words in this book, "'Free' is a magical word in retailing." I also ignored two other retailing tenets in my effort to keep operations simple:

1. Perception of a bargain is more important than reality.
2. Listening to customers is vital.

I also should have brought in more non-book items to sell since their profit margins were higher than books, but I had mostly limited such sidelines to dolls and stuffed animals only relating to books. Also, perhaps, I should have ordered more from publishers directly instead of relying mostly on wholesalers. The profit margin from a publisher was higher, but it was a slower process and more time-consuming. Again, my excuse was the store was basically a one woman operation, and I had to take shortcuts where I could. Perhaps, if I had hired more people, the store might have made more money — or maybe it would have ended in the red, instead of my not owing anybody any money when I closed. I'll never know for sure.

Larry and I had often talked of moving the mystery section to a much larger space in the back room. We planned to have a bookcase open up as a hidden door and add accessories such as a steamer trunk and wingback chairs that Sherlock Holmes might have felt comfortable sitting in, but the time had never seemed quite right. It definitely would have attracted interest but would also have required more staff.

I felt, too, that I'd gotten a lot of things right for the almost twenty years the store was in business.

There was also the dubious consolation that I wasn't alone in having to give up my store. According to Wikipedia, along with the fictionalized Meg Ryan character, 40% of independent booksellers in the United

States closed their doors in the years between 1995 and 2000!

Eventually in 2002, a nail salon owner made an offer on the building, which we accepted.

34. Last Words From My Best Customer

The Book Nook's TALE OF MR. MCGREGOR'S Writing Contest proved very successful. Teachers assigned the contest as a homework project and 480 fourth and fifth grade children re-wrote THE TALE OF PETER RABBIT from the point of view of the villain, Mr. McGregor.

Readers of the original tale associated with Peter Rabbit's terror when he was chased by Mr. McGregor for eating the farmer's vegetables, but the re-writers easily slid into Mr. McGregor's shoes, showing how disgusted the farmer was having his hard-earned labors ruined by the rabbit. They came up with inventive reasons for Mrs. McGregor baking Peter's father in a pie, including placing the entire blame on Mrs. McGregor, and they thought up clever ways to stop Peter from ruining Mr. McGregor's garden (sneezing bombs, putting cement in the rabbit's shoes, and feeding Peter so much he got bloated and couldn't fit through the fence).

It was at the end, however, describing what happened to Mr. McGregor that the children's imaginations really soared.

- *"After chasing him for awhile he [Peter Rabbit] got away and would you believe it, he actually sued me?"*

- *"They [the rabbits] ate me out of house and home. Now I live in a shack."*

- *"I gave up farm life and became a lawyer. I have never seen him again. I do come across judges with similar personalities though."*

- *"I was arrested for animal abuse....They locked me in a room with rabbit wallpaper and fed me carrots every day."*

One inventive young author, however, implied there is a reason to suspect Mr. McGregor's alibis.

- *"That's the truth and nothing but the truth. I swear it on my lucky rabbit's foot. OOOPS!"* *

DURING the Book Nook's last few years in business, I looked forward to John, a fourth-grade teacher, stopping in practically every Saturday afternoon. As he checked out different sections of the store, we swapped information about the latest children's books we had read. With his enthusiasm, he must have turned many of his students into avid readers and future authors, as well as

---

* Adapted from one of my Book Chat columns.

helping to shape their characters. *Pay it Forward* by Catherine Ryan Hyde, was one of his favorite books. I also helped him select books for his mother. His Saturday visits ended my work week on an upbeat note.

We sometimes discussed our writing endeavors. I gave John my manuscript, *Timothy's Bedtime Monsters*. He read the picture book story to his fourth-grade students and gave it to them as an assignment. Guided by him, they wrote what they liked about it. They all were intrigued by the obnoxious sister character. They also made suggestions how to improve the story, such as more development of the sister, using similes, and using onomatopoeia—every student felt strongly about using onomatopoeia. Their advice inspired me to create a much-improved version of my story.

When the store's closing became imminent, John's girlfriend Donna, and her daughter, who sometimes accompanied him, came in without him one day and snapped numerous pictures of the store to put in a booklet they were creating for his birthday. The pictures have faded over the years, but the long poem they wrote for him still exists, reflecting his love of the Book Nook. It was a takeoff on the Beatle's song, *Let it be, Let it be.*

> *When I find myself in times of trouble*
> *Judy Hoff's store comes to me.*
> *Speaking words of wisdom*
> *Come and read, come and read.*

They showed John lamenting about the store's approaching last days:

> *Oh, what will I do when the*
> *Book Nook's not there any more?*

And again:

> *Get back, you rebel*
> *Get back, Jude*
> *With your low-heeled shoes*
> *And your high-necked sweater.*
> *Get back to selling books to John.*

A couple of weeks before my final day, June 9, 2002, John came to the beginning of my closing sale. I asked him to write in my Farewell Book. Several other customers had already written moving tributes there, including many teachers, but he refused. He said he wanted to take his time, and put his sentiments about the store and me in a letter. I was afraid his busy life might interfere with his good intentions and urged him again to write in my book while he was here, but he was adamant.

I should have had more faith in him because he did return a few days later, not only with his hand-written letter but also with a gift of a quill pen and holder, symbolic encouragement for the writing I was looking forward to having time to do in retirement. He left before I had a chance to read his letter, but that turned out to be fortunate since I might not have been able to hide my first reaction to it.

He started by saying he was puzzled by what drew him so often to the Book Nook, and mentioned his girlfriend's suggestion that I was like one of the Greek Sirens luring him into the store.

Yes! Greek Siren. I liked the sound of that.

But, he went on to write, no, Greek Siren wasn't it. Instead, maybe the attraction of the store was connected to the desk where I usually sat. The four pillars around the sales area reminded him of Lucy's booth, "Psychiatric Help, 5 cents" from Schultz's Charlie Brown cartoons. John had observed people often told me their problem in between purchases.

Okay, not as exciting as being compared to a Greek Siren, but I'd take it.

Except that really wasn't it either. It suddenly came to him, he wrote, why he enjoyed coming to the store so often. It was, he said in triumph, because I possessed the same sterling qualities as his grandmother. I reminded him so much of his beloved grandmother.

His grandmother?

His *grandmother*!

It took me a few days to recognize the comparison as the huge honor he had intended.

35. Last Words From My Worst Customer

(Email to my mother in early June 2002)

I hadn't expected such an outpouring of good wishes from so many people.

My customers have outdone themselves thanking me for the Book Nook. In letters to me, in the Farewell Book, and in person, they mention how much they've enjoyed our conversations, how they appreciated my help in suggesting books, how amazed they always were that orders arrived so quickly, and how their children picked out their first books in the store. As for the Book Nook itself, they refer to it as "a haven," "a treasure house," and even a "magical place."

FINALLY in the spring of 2002, we had a firm buyer for the building.

With the news of the Book Nook's closing, customers flocked in to say good-bye—and to take advantage of the drastic price reductions. An article in

The Daily Gazette about the Book Nook captured the store's charm, relayed customer raves, and effectively advertised the Book Nook's impending demise. I couldn't help reflecting that such a favorable article would have been a terrific boost to the store's sales if it had happened in any of the other nineteen years, while the store was actually in business.

As customers piled up their bargains at the register, they lamented how much they were going to miss the store. Encouraging them to write their farewells in a large, blank book, I was amazed by their eloquence— *The best profit this store has, is not in the balance sheet but in our hearts.* On the whole, instead of dwelling on their own sadness at the store's shutting its doors, they emphasized how grateful they were that the store had existed and wished me well in the future.

Before these comments, I had feared being mired in misery once my identity was no longer connected to the bookstore. Empty days without seeing stimulating company and lack of access to any book that struck my fancy loomed before me. Gone would be my excuse for not cleaning my house or not doing mundane chores— I hadn't sent out a Christmas card in almost two decades and probably wouldn't be able to justify avoiding it any longer.

To prevent sinking into depression, I'd determinedly been repeating like a mantra at least twice a day since March the following:

*Once the store closes, I will have the opportunity
to move on to new adventures. For the first time in
years I will be able to go out for lunch with friends. I
will finally have time to write, and who knows what
other wonderful, exciting opportunities are waiting
for me.*

I didn't really believe in mantras, but was desperate enough to try anything, and to my surprise, it turned out you can reprogram your mind to a certain extent. I did begin to feel marginally better about closing and realized that a bookstore-less life might be bearable after all.

However, it was the outpouring of good wishes from customers that really uplifted me and caused me to genuinely look forward to the future. Instead of feeling a failure for being driven out of a business by mega-bookstores and Amazon, thanks to my Farewell Book, individual letters of appreciation, plus everyone's good wishes, I began to recognize that the Book Nook had actually made a valuable contribution to the community.

I began looking forward to the future.

Although I'd always contended all bookstore customers are superior to the customers in other retail stores, my Book Nook customers were a particularly kind, patient, and stimulating lot. Every time the door opened I had looked up eagerly expecting to see an old friend or to make a new one.

After almost two decades in business, I could count the customers I disliked on one hand. Of this number, however, only one person caused my breath to catch, my hands to clench together, and my knees to lock the minute her short, sturdy frame stalked into the store. Alternatively dressed in either a brown or a steel gray creased linen suit with matching scuffed low-heeled pumps, she made sure every one within hearing distance knew she had a grudge against small stores. If the store were empty, she'd stalk around muttering under her breath until another customer entered. Then, she would pick up a book and announce loudly that she'd seen the identical book on the sale table for a lot less money at K-Mart or at Barnes and Noble.

When she first began coming in, I tried to be pleasant. Despite my efforts, she became more negative with each visit. She went into tirades, complaining about my store, the other awful stores on Upper Union Street, and the terrible world in general.

My responses to her descended into monosyllabic grunts; then complete silence.

A few days before I shut my doors for good, *Ms. Ill Will* marched in during a surprisingly quiet time and selected her first purchase ever, a bestselling paperback. It was 70% off. She asked if the store was definitely closing. I refrained from pointing to the large sign that everybody else saw in the window and simply replied, "Yes

While I rang up the sale, an automatic "How are you doing?" spilled out of my mouth. I instantly wanted to take it back, but it was too late. She proceeded to tell me in great detail about how her leg was paining her, how it had kept her up all night, and how the doctors couldn't help her.

Since I was experiencing a knee problem—a torn meniscus—I reluctantly began to feel some sympathy. I heard my mother's voice echoing in my mind, lecturing that I should be friendlier toward her, that she was probably in constant pain, which would make anyone cranky.

"I'm so sorry."

She narrowed her brown eyes into slits and snapped. "What do you care? You don't even like me!"

I wish I could report about my speedy retort. A Bill Clinton line delivered without his sincerity, "True, but I do feel your pain." might have moved me out of the wimp category.

Unfortunately, I was speechless.

She snatched up my precious *Farewell Book*. "What's more, I'm going to write in here."

No! No! No! Not my precious book with all those wonderful comments from so many wonderful customers. Please, please, please, don't destroy it.

I didn't dare grab it back from her, fearing a tug-of-war might rip it in two.

I envisioned her scrawling down terrible insults and perhaps writing over some of the extravagant praise. The fierce expression on her face made me afraid that she might even begin shredding it. The page she opened contained a special message from my very dear friend, Phyllis, who had owned the gift shop next door.

Remain calm. Don't let her see how much the book means to you.

After spending an agonizing amount of time thinking, she finally scrawled a brief message, ending with a flourish.

I hoped it wasn't a profanity.

She set the pen down carefully and then slammed the book shut.

Whew! At least she hadn't destroyed the book or even someone else's comments, but what poisonous thought had she written down?

Not wanting to give her the satisfaction of knowing that I cared, I fooled around on the computer, checking one of my last orders for customers, but she had my number. "Bet you're dying to know what I wrote." she said.

I shrugged.

She laughed evilly, turned, and strutted out.

I am not a paranoid person. Not me. However, I did wait a good five minutes to make sure she wouldn't come back and peep in one of the windows and catch me reading what she'd written. To make doubly sure, I casually strolled to the front windows and checked that she was safely entering another store across the street, probably to torture that shopkeeper. I rushed back to my desk, grabbed my precious book, and hurriedly flipped to her comment.

Thank goodness, it wasn't a blatant slur that would ruin the book. It might even be read as a goodwill message. Yet, I knew it was a subtle dig.

I couldn't help it; I had to laugh.

She'd written: *"Better luck next time."*

36. THE LAST DAY

(Part of email to my daughters, both then working in New York City - 6/8/2002)

Last day was yesterday!

I sold books all day at a mere $1.50 per paperback and $3 per hardcover but did get rid of a lot. Not enough! There are still loads of adult books to pack up. Children's books are down to two boxes. I will donate   them all. Lots of teachers in, buying for their classrooms, which I was happy to see. Also, M.K. bought forty paperbacks for the jail. She volunteers at their library. Then, she discovered poetry books and brought over ten more. She claimed they were so popular, they cannot keep them in the library. She explained many prisoners are dyslexic and the only writing they can do is to painstakingly copy the poetry when they send letters. I gave her those.

I gave all my old customers one or two books, and sometimes more.

Yesterday about 3 p.m., it suddenly hit me again how lucky I've been all these years to have had this wonderful bookstore, and I wanted to cry, big gulping sobs, but managed to keep the tears back until the last customer left at 5:15. Dad kept me company from noon until then.

It was a very tiring day. There is a mammoth job still ahead of packing up books to donate and disposing of nineteen years' worth of clutter — let alone bookcases and other furniture. Many of the original bookcases are going to Laura. She will have the equivalent of a bookstore in her basement.

I wish everybody could have such an outpouring of good wishes. Even granting for the natural overabundance of emotion on such an occasion, I feel in a small way like that Jimmy Stewart character in IT'S A WONDERFUL LIFE! The movie they drag out every Christmas. The one where he discovered his life had meaning after all. I never realized before how much the store has meant to so many people.

I am so moved, Gin and Trish, you wanted to give me a party, but feel the right decision to back out of it; it would just be too much, and in my last two weeks I have received one accolade after another.

It's been more than enough.

Afterword: The Legend

EVEN though the Book Nook has been closed now for over two decades, I still encounter former customers at the Niskayuna Co-op who moan about how much they miss it.

I miss it too, but people's memories of the store astound me. The more time passes, the more the Book Nook has metamorphosized into a booklovers' paradise, a calming haven free from the stresses of the frantic real world; shelved with the perfect selection of books, each title more intriguing than the next.

What's more, I am now idealized as the ultimate bookseller, one who had read every book on the shelves, who knew all details about every author, and one who could place the perfect title in a shopper's hands every time.

Not possible, but who am I to disillusion anyone?

I did love it.

ABOUT THE AUTHOR

JUDY HOFF cannot believe that she is in her eighties already! She spends much of her time transporting her grandsons to their activities. She warns them she is keeping a tally so that in a few years when their mother and their aunt take away her car keys, and both boys have their drivers' licenses, she will expect them to drive her everywhere.

Swimming forty-five minutes every other day in the JCC Schenectady Pool, Judy often feels transformed back to her sixteen-year-old self in Amagansett, New York, where she loved swimming in the Atlantic Ocean at the end of her street.

You can contact Judy at *judyshoffbooks@gmail.com.*

At *judyshoffbooks.com*, you will:

- find details about bookstore signings for *HOW MUCH ARE THESE FREE BOOKS?*

- read 21 hand-selling tips from Judy's article in *American Bookseller Magazine*